PLAIN STYLE

Techniques for Simple, Concise, Emphatic Business Writing

RICHARD LAUCHMAN

amacom

American Management Association

New York • Atlanta • Boston • Chicago • Kansas City • San Francisco • Washington, D.C.
Brussels • Toronto • Mexico City

This book is available at a special
discount when ordered in bulk quantities.
For information, contact Special Sales Department,
AMACOM, a division of American Management Association,
1601 Broadway, New York, NY 10019.

This publication is designed to provide accurate and authoritative information in regard to the subject matter covered. It is sold with the understanding that the publisher is not engaged in rendering legal, accounting, or other professional service. If legal advice or other expert assistance is required, the services of a competent professional person should be sought.

Library of Congress Cataloging-in-Publication Data

Lauchman, Richard.
    Plain style : techniques for simple, concise, emphatic business
writing / Richard Lauchman.
        p.   cm.
    ISBN 0-8144-7852-2
    1. Business writing.   I. Title.
HF5718.3.L38   1993
808'.06665—dc20

                                                                93-4324
                                                                CIP

Printing number

10   9   8   7   6   5   4

To my parents,
William and Pauline,
with love and gratitude
and
To Elif,
who completes the circle of one

Contents

Part Two: Techniques for Conciseness and Emphasis 27

On Being Concise 29

On Being Emphatic 63

Introduction

If you believe that a toothpick should be called a toothpick, and not a *wood interdental stimulator*, and if you would rather read *We think* than *It is at this point in time the opinion of the committee that*, then you are three-quarters of the way to writing simply, and the advice you find here will help.

Everyone agrees that simple, straightforward writing saves time, wins customers, and prevents expensive misunderstandings. Complicated writing does the opposite—and while the stuff of business, science, and regulation isn't simple, writing should be. $E = MC^2$, for example, expresses a mind-boggling concept in a breathtakingly simple way. Too often, however, business writing races in the other direction. When the writer means *We must define and rank our marketing goals* but writes, *Marketing stratagems must be definitized and prioritized*, he is complicating a simple idea.

Too much of today's business writing is needlessly difficult to understand. And certainly, in a world that grows more complex by the moment, simplicity of style becomes increasingly important. This book shows you how to strip the complexity from your writing—how to write in a way that not only satisfies the rules and is creditable to your organization but is clear on first reading, contains no clutter, and sounds remarkably like reasonable speech. Such writing is called concise, and it's what good business writing should be.

Plain Style

In business writing, style should be invisible. It should never be an issue. It must never call attention to itself, never intrude on the ideas themselves. Most important, it must never create needless complexity. Every expression should be functional, like the two-by-fours used (and hidden) in the framing of a house, not displayed or flaunted, like the gorgeously grained mahogany used in paneling.

Plain style is what results when the writer has a clear idea and decides to convey that idea. Not to express it, but to *convey* it. There is a

1

huge difference. *Cunctator* expresses something, but does it convey a meaning to you? Would *procrastinator* better enable you to understand? *Supports the conclusion that* certainly expresses something. But what? Would *proves* be a better word? Only the writer knows. Only the writer knows whether he means *proves*—or *suggests, indicates, confirms, reveals, demonstrates, implies,* or *underscores.*

Plain style begins with a commitment to convey. Writers who wish to "express" themselves will do well to write poems, novels, and letters from the heart, where ambiguity and obliqueness have their place. There is no room for ambiguity in the kind of writing where money changes hands.

Writing Can Easily Be Simplified

This may surprise people who deplore the lack of "language skills" in business and government, but writing a clear thought in plain words is well within the ability of professionals. We are hardly doomed to read such Byzantine statements as this:

> Purification of unliquidated obligations is essential for the early identification and correction of invalid obligation amounts to ensure full and effective fund utilization.
>
> *—by a midlevel professional at a federal agency*

Over the last decade, I've presented hundreds and hundreds of writing workshops to professionals in all areas of business and government. In the classroom, after some coaching, participants write well. What's important to understand is that I give them *permission to write simply* and then work on two issues that empower writers to give themselves this permission.

First, I need to remind writers of what actually happens in the interchange we call reading. Often a radical adjustment in thinking is necessary here, as writers are plagued by a host of complicating assumptions. For example, many people feel compelled to begin with background, forgetting that readers of business documents scan until they find the main point; many use big words, forgetting that they themselves prefer to read little ones; many forget that it is the reader (not the writer) who decides whether an expression is clear. Well before I suggest technique, I need to remind writers of how they themselves read business documents—what their expectations are, how their reading changes to editing when they spot errors, and how commas, parentheses, and dashes suggest differing levels of importance. Only one who understands how people actually read is able to write well.

Second, because of the way English is taught in the United States—a way that can be described as inconsistent at best—I need to act as a sort of lay exorcist, casting out demons of dogma and superstition. Nearly every writer is haunted by a phantom catechism of don'ts—Don't split an infinitive, Don't use the passive voice, Don't start a sentence with *Because*, Don't use personal pronouns, Don't use parentheses, Don't use dashes, Don't end a sentence with a preposition, Don't write one-sentence paragraphs, Don't repeat words, Don't put a comma after the last thing in a series—and dozens more, some of which are truly bizarre (e.g., Don't put a comma before *however*, Never begin a sentence with *If*, and Don't use the same sentence structure twice in a row). Unless I help writers distinguish dogma from practical usage, they will continue to feel uncomfortable with plain language and will inadvertently complicate their writing.

What Makes Business Writing Needlessly Complex

When writers leave the workshops, they are capable of conveying clear ideas. But merely that—merely capable. When they return to their desks, other complications erupt, and their good writing goes the way of the lamb to the slaughter. It is not enough for writers to give themselves permission to write simply—their managers must also give this permission, and many managers unwittingly deny it.

This happens in the minefield known as the review process. Manager after manager handles the document; manager after manager explodes the text. Each successive manager, believing he's not doing his job unless he improves the writing in some way (or merely wishing to impose a personal stamp), alters a phrase, substitutes a word, adds a sentence, or qualifies an expression. While some of the changes are useful, most are unnecessary and many are actually harmful. The honest and simple *policy* is changed to the less precise *procedure* and then to the imprecise but impressive *protocol*. Commas and semicolons are inserted where they have no business being; abbreviations that require no explanation are laboriously explained; *if* blows up into *in the event that*. Clearly, it makes no difference how well a professional writes if her managers complicate the text.

Managers justify even the most impractical changes by saying, "That's the way we do it here." Thus, a writer at FCC finds his *cellular telephone used in an airport* contorted into *airport mobile cellular unit*. A writer at a bank finds her clear sentence *We must revise our procedures for redeeming outdated checks* twisted into the confusing and misleading *We must revise our outdated check redemption procedures*. When the document arrives at the Office of General Counsel for final review, any surviving *dog* becomes a *canine*. Personal pronouns are beheaded without trial, *retroactively* explodes into *nunc pro tunc*, and the warheads of *pursuant to* and *aforementioned* are installed to make the text properly bristle.

The thing to remember is that these changes occur without regard to the document's purpose, occasion, or audience. They occur because "That's the way we do it here," which is to say from unexamined tradition. If we want to improve business writing, we must start by getting rid of the senseless traditions that complicate it. If managers gave professionals permission to write well—insisting on simplicity and having the restraint to leave well enough alone—the clarity of business writing would double overnight.

Why a Consensus Is Essential

To achieve plain style, writers and managers at all levels of an organization must agree that inflated writing is counterproductive, irresponsible, and unkind to the reader. Without a consensus on this point, simplicity stands no chance, and writers will continue to "express" themselves at the reader's expense. Here are some examples of sentences expressing something or other:

> The previous staffing requirements were adjusted to recognize that the idealized fractionalization and time phasing of communication support skilled personnel desired by proposal managers will often not be possible.
>
> —*by a midlevel professional at a Fortune 100 company*

> The undersigned has devised a narrative that delineates chronological aspects of a given environment, twice pronounced in differing configurations, of which one is decidedly superior to its counterpart.
>
> —*by a midlevel professional at a federal agency*

> A proactive position vis-à-vis the escalation of the matter of ongoing sudden outage interference with the making of long-distance indials by customers has been taken.
>
> —*by a customer service representative at a telecommunications company*

Such a monstrous "style"—cut off from the rhythms of ordinary speech and utterly alien to reason—is learned nowhere but in the workplace. No one learns to write that way in college or graduate school. Such infected writing results from the very contagious virus known as "That's our style." Must it be so? How long will we continue to pretend that such writing does anything other than waste time and money?

The plain truth is that as long as managers and executives tolerate bloated and pretentious language, they are tacitly encouraging it. As long as outmoded or poorly conceived formats dictate complexity, language will be complex. This is bad for business: Contracts are lost, customers outraged, deadlines missed, sensitive intelligence misunderstood, and time squandered. It is in the workplace that impractical style has evolved, and it is in the workplace, on the desks of those who review and sign documents, that the return to common sense must begin.

About This Book

I firmly believe that most professionals have all the skill required to write clearly. But I also believe that if skill is a seed, then judgment is the soil. Planted in unhealthy soil, even the most robust acorn will give rise to something spindly and grotesque. Isn't it self-evident that anyone who can write *had a pronounced negative effect on* can just as easily write *damaged*? His skill does not prevent him from using the simpler expression. His judgment does.

And so it seemed to me that a good book on conciseness must begin by delving underneath the words on the page—the *results* of the thinking—and seek to understand the origin of those words, the thinking itself, the attitudes and assumptions that form the soil of judgment.

The first part of this book, "The Practical Writer," prepares the soil. It suggests ways to think about writing—certain assumptions we should make—that can greatly simplify the way we choose to express an idea. The second part of the book presents a number of techniques that make writing concise and emphatic. The primary focus here is on individual sentences, for it is in the sentence that style begins and in the sentence that we can begin our return to saying precisely what we mean.

He and *she* have been used interchangeably throughout. I find this practice preferable to having one version of the book for women and another version for men.

Definitions

bad faith   In writing, any "agenda" other than honest and direct communication. Bad faith is present when the writer uses big words not because they are precise but to impress the reader; bad faith is present when the writer chooses to conceal his meaning, as well as when he intentionally misleads. Bad faith rots writing whenever the writer puts himself first; in a nutshell, bad faith results from an attitude: *Here, reader, see whether you can figure out what I mean.* No degree of skill with language will overcome it.

big words   Words that complicate reading because they are simply more than the meaning requires. *Prognosticate* and *perambulate*, for example, are big words if the writer means "predict" and "wander." But a word doesn't need to have lots of syllables to be considered "big." *Limn* and *eloign* are brief, but if the reader doesn't know what they mean, they are big in the sense of being pretentious. Ultimately, readers decide whether the words are inflated: *syzygy* isn't a big word for astonomers, but it's a whopper for nonexperts.

clarity   In writing, a *reader's* verdict. An expression may be clear to a writer, but if it is unclear to the reader, then it is unclear. The simple sentence *Thinking clearly matters* looks clear to the writer, who wishes it to mean "Clear thinking matters." The reader could easily understand the meaning to be "Clearly, thinking matters." In this case, the sentence isn't clear; the true test of clarity is whether the reader understands the writer's intended meaning—and understands it on the first reading.

common sense   In writing, an attitude that results in simple, practical expressions. Common sense argues that if the writer wishes to convey *The audit is scheduled for tomorrow*, then he use the word *audit* and not *inspection, review, analysis, determination,* or some other vague word. The reader too has common sense, and when she reads, *Doctors are feeding him intravenously, and he's trying very hard to eat himself,* her common sense may save the writer's meaning—but then again it may not. The writer is encouraged to use his own.

complexity   In writing, an evil, and not a necessary one. What one is writing about may be terribly complex, but the expression of that

7

complexity should be simple. *It is suggested that the attempt to manifest the traits, mannerisms, and idiosyncratic proclivities of another is neither rational nor necessary* is a complex expression of a profound thought. *Be yourself* is profoundly simple. Good writers let the complexity inherent in the subject be the only complexity in the writing.

complicate   To make a simple idea complex.

concise   Describes a sentence that is clear on first reading and contains no superfluous word. The sentence *We need new policy guidelines* is brief, but it is not concise, because it is unclear. *We need guidelines for the new policy* or *We need new guidelines for the policy* would be concise. Note that each revision contains two more words than the ambiguous original. Clarity demands the additional words; the key to being concise is to eliminate unnecessary words. Thus, it is concise to say, in six words, that Mr. Green is *an advocate for the mentally ill* and patently silly to call him, in four words, *a mentally ill advocate*.

dogma   In writing, those conventions of usage that fly in the face of common sense because they deny how the language is actually used. "Avoid the passive voice" is an example of dogma, as are "never split an infinitive" and "never end a sentence with a preposition." Dogma is based not in logic but in unexamined tradition, and it serves no purpose but to make expressions unnecessarily awkward and complex. See *Pedant*.

good faith   In writing, the absence of any "agenda" other than simple, honest, responsive, and courteous communication. One who practices good faith in writing has, in effect, an "invisible" style—no quirks of expression, big words, or needless complexity interfere with the reading. Instead, well-chosen words provide effortless access to the ideas.

good writer   In business writing, one who puts the reader first. Putting the reader first requires that we write the kind of sentences we ourselves would find easy to understand.

"I was taught that"   (1) An honest call for the clarification of a usage; (2) a defensive excuse muttered by a pedant who's been caught red-handed in the act of writing something like *The undersigned encloses herewith the report which up was looked for which you asked in which are stated fourth-quarter expenses up with which we cannot put.*

pedant   One who complicates writing out of a stubborn adherence to superstitions about language (dogma, or false rules). Pedants believe, because they were once taught so, that many ordinary usages are "wrong"; the pedant, for whom correctness is more important than communication, insists that it's "improper English" to start a sentence with *Because*, repeat words, or use *I* in formal writing. No cure for this condition is known, but where pedants manage the writing of others, the seeds of plain style do not grow.

Plain Style　The absence of "style"; a way of writing in which style calls no attention to itself. Only when the words are transparent—when nothing intrudes, distracts, or confuses—will the reader have effortless access to the ideas. This is the appropriate style in business and technical writing.

simple　Describes writing that is easy to understand; relates to the expression of ideas, and is always a strength. *They discussed the issue yesterday* is simple. *The parties dialogued apropos the matter on a previous occasion* is not simple; besides being imprecise, it is unnecessarily complex and difficult to understand.

simplistic　Describes oversimplified thinking; relates to the thinking itself, not to the expression of the thought, and is always a weakness. Most generalizations (for example, "Never split an infinitive") reflect simplistic thought. In business writing, oversimplified thinking manifests itself as wishfulness, as in *We would have won the contract if we had bid $10,000 less*, when actually there were many other reasons why the contract was lost. Relevant experience may have been inadequate, for example, or the organization's reputation may have been shoddy, or—perhaps equally important—the proposal itself may have been sloppily written.

style　The by-product of the writer's decisions. Joe, deciding that he wishes to convey an idea, writes, *We need four butterfly bolts*. Stansfield, deciding that he'll conform to tradition and make the idea sound more, well, "professional," writes, *This office is in necessitation of four (4) butterfly bolts*. And there you have style. Which would you rather read?

ultimate reader　The person or persons for whom the document is ultimately intended, used when necessary to distinguish this reader from the managers who also read and review documents. Not to be understood as an ideal (clairvoyant) reader. In the eternal scenario involving writer, reader, and page, this is the individual who counts.

ultra-pedant　A pedant who happens to be wrong. Ultra-pendants take an ill-advised "rule" like "You can't end a sentence with a preposition," get it backwards, and insist, "You can't start a sentence with a preposition." A common ultra-pendant rule is "You never put a comma after the last thing in a series." The ultra-pendant therefore writes, *Be sure to include your name, age, sex and salary requirements*. In business and government, most ultra-pedants write very little but extensively edit the writing of others.

Wonderland   Where all readers go when the writer needlessly complicates an expression. When, for example, the writer intends to say that
high-altitude winds may bring lethal radioactivity to the United States,
yet writes, *Some of these deaths may be exported to the U.S. via the Trade
Winds*, the reader is in Wonderland. Most often, it is not so entertaining a place to visit.

PART ONE

The Practical Writer

The Problem With "Style"

When I use a word, it means just what I choose it to mean—
neither more nor less.

—Humpty Dumpty, in *Through the Looking Glass*

Mr. Dumpty would find "style" to his liking. The word has been used so promiscuously that it now signifies nearly every aspect of writing—and when a person uses it, you can never be sure what he's talking about.

Style can mean whatever you want it to mean. Customer Service Departments give employees "style sheets" that suggest phrases to be used and phrases to be avoided (so certain phrases must be part of style). Most style sheets indicate the preferred format and typeface to be used as well (so format and typeface must be part of style). Corporations and government agencies distribute "style guides" that dictate the use of numbers, hyphens, capitalization, and just about any other aspect of standard usage you can imagine (so standard English must be part of style). *The Chicago Manual of Style* covers punctuation, grammar, and mechanics, so these must be part of style as well.

Style surely covers convention, too. The great majority of style guides feel an almost evangelical call to remind us, for example, not to split infinitives. A major telecommunications company's Proposal Preparation Guide puts the matter this way:

> A split infinitive occurs when an adverb appears between *to* and the infinitive it governs. NEVER USE SPLIT INFINITIVES!!!

Style can apply to spelling, as some authorities insist that *cancelling*, *travelling*, and *focussing* are "correct style," while others prefer *canceling*, *traveling*, and *focusing*. Some newspapers have dropped the letters *ue* from words like *demagogue*, *catalogue*, and *dialogue*; *The Washington Post* dropped the final *e* from *employee* (*employe* was their style of spelling) and then, in response to a surprising amount of mail, put it back on.

Style covers everything from abbreviations to symbols. Nothing is sacrosanct; no aspect of writing escapes. Style reaches out and lays its clammy fingers even on the number of a noun! A *Fortune* 100 company's Editorial Style Manual claims, for example, that "personnel" is *singular*. An example of its "correct" use—the example in the style guide—is this:

All personnel is required to report to work by 8:30 A.M.

In my word processing software, style doesn't refer to any of these; it refers, instead, to my options of italicizing, underscoring, boldfacing, subscripting, or doing a number of other things to make the words stand out. So graphics must be part of style.

What *isn't* style? And how useful is a word that encompasses phrasing, format, typeface, punctuation, capitalization, abbreviations, the use of numbers, the use of hyphens, the meanings of words, the "correctness" of words, the spellings of words, whether you split an infinitive, whether you use personal pronouns, all of the above, none of the above, some of the above? When you say *style*, it means just what you choose it to mean—neither more nor less.

If style refers to everything, then it refers to nothing in particular. But in the practical world, where our goal is to communicate to others, words with loose definitions have no place; they reduce us to making noise when we're trying to make sense. And when a manager tells an employee, "Letters for my signature must be written in my style," we have an enigma parading as a sentence.

Toward a Definition of Style

If we are to discuss style in any meaningful way, we must first rescue the word from the wilderness of vague reference and assign it a precise meaning. A clear (and very useful) definition is possible, but it will make sense only if we agree on ten precepts.

First, let's agree that we are discussing business writing and nothing else. We are concerning ourselves with reports, proposals, memos, letters, and so forth: documents (1) that are written to make a point and (2) that the reader, in his day-to-day work, is obliged to read and understand. We are not concerning ourselves with documents that the reader chooses to read (novels, magazine articles, love letters, poems, and so forth), but only with the ones that he must read.

Second, let's agree that the nature of reading varies widely. We bring differing expectations to different kinds of documents: We expect a mystery story to keep us in suspense, but we expect the opposite from a memo. We tolerate and even enjoy ambiguity in a poem, but we expect clear language in a contract. In a letter from an old friend, we ignore errors in grammar and spelling—but do we ignore such errors when we read a sales letter or a proposal?

Third, let's agree that business documents receive a "functional" reading. The expectations we bring to a business document differ from those we bring to any other kind of writing. We read not for entertainment but to discover what the writer wants us to do or to know. Therefore, we expect to encounter ideas, not to have to decipher stilted, awkward, or needlessly complex expressions—and certainly we expect to understand a sentence the first time we read it. In addition, we expect economy of expression: Business writing isn't poetry, and we do not treasure the writer's choice of words. If we encounter *notwithstanding the fact that*, we convert the sense to "although." Finally, we expect the document to make a point: Business writing isn't detective fiction, and if the point isn't in the first paragraph, we stop reading the sentences in order. We begin to scan.

Fourth, let's agree that there are rules and conventions governing the language and refer to the entire body of these rules and conventions as standard English. Those aspects of writing governed by standard English include grammar, punctuation, capitalization, the customary usage of words, and the spelling of words. We can agree that standard English is not fixed; we can agree that the language is in perpetual flux; we can agree that there are reasonable disputes about usage. What's important is that we accept this basic premise: There is a shared code that fosters communication, and the further one strays from that code, the less effective (clear, creditable, persuasive) one's writing becomes.

Fifth, let's agree that business writing must conform to standard English. Would anyone argue with this point? The purpose of business writing is to inform or to persuade, not to mystify. Business writing isn't experimental fiction, and writers who take liberties with standard spelling, grammar, and punctuation not only impose an undue burden on the reader but risk being judged as incompetent. In the competitive environment, credibility is a priceless commodity; when customers encounter sloppy writing, their reaction is swift and severe. You would certainly (and understandably) hesitate to award a contract to any company whose proposal was infested with errors in basic English. The subtextual message of sloppiness is inferred by all: The writer is negligent and inattentive (at best), or ignorant and unable (at worst). Such a response may not be noble, but it is quick and sure.

Sixth, let's agree that if sentences are (for any reason) incorrect, then style is not the issue. One who writes, "The problem with these proposals are that they are incomplete" is guilty not of poor style but of poor grammar. One who writes, "The policy will enable us to accomodate the needs of all employees" is guilty not of poor style but of poor spelling. In a sentence such as "Our Senior auditor Donald Marks, visited the Banks headquarters on May 18," the issue is not style; punctuation and capitalization are simply incorrect.

Seventh, let's agree that so long as people conform to standard English, they are entitled to write in any way they prefer. Let's see where this liberalism gets us. Joe can write, "The advertising campaign must be simplified." Stansfield is free to write, "The product recognition program is in need of a substantial amelioration enhancement." Both sentences conform to the conventions of standard English; both are, in an abstract universe, identical in terms of "perfection."

Eighth, let's agree that in the practical world both the writer and his readers pay a price for needless complexity. While Stansfield's style is perfectly legitimate, it is a style best reserved for his Great American Novel, his diary, his poetry, or his mumbling to himself. In the world of work, the result of Stansfield's "style" is (1) Stansfield's risking a reputation as a bully and (2) communication ruptured, trust lost, time wasted, money squandered.

Ninth, let's agree that we would rather read Joe's sentence than Stansfield's sentence. Anyone who would rather read Stansfield's sentence is excused from writing in the business environment and should go to Paris, wear a black beret, frequent bistros, and revel in syllables. Joe's sentence is simple and embodies everything that is good about writing: It is effortless reading.

Tenth, let's agree that the Golden Rule is a good one to apply to writing and that if we prefer to read Joe's sentence, then we should write Joe's sentence. Here we see the first glimmers of what style truly is, because anyone who could write a sentence like Stansfield's could—merely that, merely *could*—write a sentence like Joe's.

"Style takes its final shape more from attitudes of mind than from principles of composition," Mr. Strunk wrote succinctly in *The Elements of Style*. This is the heart of the matter: Anyone who writes like Stansfield chooses to do so.

Since Stansfield could, if he'd wanted to, have written Joe's sentence, his skill with language isn't the issue. His judgment is the issue. If business writing is to improve, we must understand that style is best understood to be the by-product of the writer's judgment. Stansfield's style manifests his judgment; his judgment, in turn, is based on his attitudes (about words, about himself, about the occasion, and toward his reader) and on his assumptions about the interaction called reading. If we can agree that, in business writing, any style that interferes with readability is a bad style, then Stansfield's style is a poor one. But it is also easily improved. All that is required of Stansfield is that he (1) practice good faith in writing and (2) adopt more practical assumptions about what his readers need.

We'll turn now to what Mr. Strunk called attitudes of mind: those assumptions that form the soil of judgment.

Practical Thinking

To write in plain style, we need to think about writing in a certain way (a way that might be called practical). Our assumptions about writing—what it should look and sound like, what it should accomplish, and so forth—not only manifest themselves in every sentence we write, but they dictate style. The quitchweed seed will produce quitchweed; the acorn gives rise to the oak. Planted in mud, they both die. And if our assumptions about writing are off the mark, then our skill with language is meaningless. We will write complex and impractical stuff.

Certain assumptions complicate style; others foster simplicity. Here are the ones that foster simplicity. Make them your own.

1 A good writer works hard so that the reader won't have to.

Writing is easy. Writing well requires effort. A document that is easy to write will usually be imprecise and difficult to understand. It is easy, for example, for the writer to toss out *Modifications to the text are needed in order for there to be a lessened opportunity for miscomprehension*. It requires more effort to pick precise words and engineer them into the right order: *To minimize the chance of misunderstanding, we must clarify the policy.* Make things easy for the reader.

In brutally practical terms, if a writer spends 15 minutes on a document, but a dozen readers must spend 10 minutes each deciphering it (and calling the writer to ask her what she meant), then the communication costs 135 minutes. If the writer spends 30 minutes on the document, simplifying it so that the dozen readers need to spend only 2 minutes each, then the communication costs only 54 minutes. This very conservative example should suggest an important point: In a world where time and money equate, the responsible writer takes the time to be clear.

2 The reader reads the words, not the mind.

Your reader isn't clairvoyant; he cannot read your mind. His only responsibility is to read what you actually write. He should never need to guess at a meaning; he should never encounter ambiguity and be forced to interpret an expression. In the sentence below, how is the estate to be divided?

> Mr. O'Connell stipulated that his estate be equally divided among his wife, his brother Kevin, and Michael and Sean, his sons.

Michael and Sean understand the sentence to mean that the estate is to be divided four ways; Mrs. O'Connell and Kevin understand it to mean that the estate is to be divided three ways. Each "interpretation" has merit. Litigation will certainly ensue, and attorneys will enjoy a handsome profit because of this poorly organized and unclear sentence.

The reader is at the writer's mercy, and when she reads, *The falling dollar will radically affect American exports,* she is forced to guess at the meaning. The writer knows that the decreased value of the dollar will *stimulate* exports, or *decrease* exports, but if he does not use those words, then the reader does not read them. The writer's knowing what he means is important—but his job is to let the reader in on the secret.

③ The reader boils things down.

When reading business documents, we reduce every expression to its simplest and essential meaning. When we encounter *in the vicinity of,* we extract the sense of "near"; when we encounter *in consideration of the fact that,* we glean the sense of "because." And we are neither fooled nor impressed by *prior to*—we dig around in those words and unearth the sense of "before." The writer should provide the simple word.

Business writing should be effortless reading. The reader of business documents should not be forced to extract, glean, or dig around in phrases like a woebegone archaeologist. Writers who believe that *at this point in time* is a professional way to say *now* are forgetting that readers refine the sense of *now* from that complex phrase. The practical writer does not make the reader work. Be concise.

④ If you give the reader a chance to misunderstand you, he will take it.

Readers are notoriously perverse this way. Presented with the least ambiguity, they will snatch a meaning other than the one the writer intended. What is the meaning of the following, innocent-looking expression?

> All of these ideas are not relevant.

The writer wants to convey that some of the ideas are irrelevant—but the reader understands that *all* of the ideas are irrelevant. Can we blame her? The second meaning haunts the expression just as surely as the first. And is the reader responsible for misinterpreting the idea? According to Assumption 2, the reader should never be faced with the need to interpret. The writer is always responsible for ambiguity. No reader should need to make sense of an idea. Making sense is the writer's job.

5   The principal goal of good writing is to convey.

Clarity alone is not the goal, because an expression can be clear and yet convey a sense other than the one the writer intended. And while vague writing provokes calls for clarification, clear writing does not. Clear writing will be accepted on its face.

> The annual USOG membership fee is $5, which includes a spouse at no extra charge.

That sentence unequivocally promises a spouse for a $5 fee. That is not what the writer means, of course. It is merely what she writes. "Oh," she says with a little wave of the hand, "readers know what I mean." The argument that readers use common sense is a reasonable one. They do. The counterarguments are more to the point: (1) Should the reader be forced into a "detective" mode? (2) Is the reader the only one who can use common sense? (3) Does the credibility of the writer count at all? (4) What are the limits of interpretation? (5) Is such writing good enough?

Business writing abounds with entertaining sentences like the ones that follow, all of which are dizzyingly "clear."

> The tornado in my opinion is an Act of God.

> You can't count the trees still standing on your fingers.

> The employee claims that rude comments were made by the water cooler on the eighth floor.

> We're confident that once you try a pair of our jeans, you'll never want to wear another.

All convey clear ideas, but none convey what the writer intended. Most readers can figure out what the writer meant to say—which is the writer's job—but what of the writer's credibility? The dull yellow gleam of inattention (or worse) glimmers in such sentences, and readers are right to look askance at the source.

⑥ The meanings of words lie in the mind, not in the dictionary.

At first glance, this idea may seem anarchic; on reflection, it may seem simplistic. But it is a law as unyielding as gravity, and writers forget it at their peril. Practically speaking, the purpose of business writing is to inform or persuade—not to enthrall, impress, or improve the vocabulary of the reader, and certainly not to hazard misunderstanding. Good writers are aware of the mischief lurking in the following sentence.

> Beginning January 1, cost analyses must be filed bimonthly, rather than monthly.

The fun begins here. The writer, believing that *bimonthly* means "every two months," presumes he had made his meaning clear. The reader, believing that *bimonthly* means "twice per month," assumes she understands the idea. Because she thinks she knows the word's meaning, she does not look it up in the dictionary.

On January 15 or 16, cost analyses begin to arrive on the surprised writer's desk. Now the fun gets going in earnest. The parties scurry to the dictionary, eager to ascertain what the word truly "means." Both meanings are there. The writer is gratified to see that the first meaning is "every two months"; the reader is relieved to see that "twice per month" follows on its heels.

And now the party is in full swing. "Look here," the writer says. "The first definition is *every two months*." The reader rounds on him. "And it also means what I thought it meant. Twice a month. It's in the dictionary!"

Knowing what the dictionary says is handy, but knowing how the reader understands a word is essential. Simple words minimize the chance that a reader will misconstrue the meaning; here, since the writer meant "every two months," the phrase *every two months* would have been simple and immediately clear.

⑦ Good writing minimizes the chance of misunderstanding.

To maximize the clarity of your writing, use the words you learned first. That's what "keep it simple" means. Rather than *prioritize desirable outcomes,* a good writer will rank goals; rather than *elucidate the protocol,* a good writer will clarify the policy. Don't erect a cathedral when a pup tent will suffice.

Unseasoned writers, especially those fresh from college and graduate school, often sleepwalk under the spell of big words. They fly to Latinate language the way iron shavings fly to a magnet; they will write *orientate* when they mean "point" and *terminate* when they mean "stop." They do so from the misconception that *utilize, bifurcate, definitize,* and *delineate* are somehow more professional than *use, divide, define,* and *outline.* The big Latinate words aren't more professional; in fact, because they require more time and guesswork from the reader, they are less so.

> Subsequent to receiving your memo, I canceled the contract.

If the writer is confident that all of his readers understand *subsequent to* to mean "after," then *subsequent to* will convey. If, however, one reader out of one hundred—for any reason, ranging from ignorance to haste—understands the phrase to mean "before," then the writer has chosen poorly. (He might be surprised to learn that five out of ten adult Americans either don't know what *subsequent to* means or confuse it with *before.*) He can insist until the very last cow comes home that *subsequent to* means "after"; he can shake a dictionary in the reader's face, point to the small print, and sputter something about a definition. His being correct on the point changes nothing: At the crucial moment, the reader has misunderstood him.

The argument that adults should know the meaning of *subsequent to* is more than elitist—it is irrelevant and vain. Work with the words you are certain your readers do know. Ultimately and inarguably, *after* is the right word if the writer means "after." It is the right word because it minimizes—not abrogates or obviates—the chance of misunderstanding. The good writer never has to resort to a dictionary to prove himself "right." The mere fact of his needing to do that proves he used bad judgment.

⑧ **The complexity of the subject should be the only complexity in the writing.**

In the complicated world of business and technical writing, where shrapnel flies disguised as *kinetic energy chunky fragments* and a research paper is formally designated a *unimolecular chemical degradation reaction study,* does it make sense to complicate further? The writer may be obliged to use a squirming noun—but no one picks his verb for him, and he alone selects his adjective. Is clarity improved when he chooses *went into sudden incendiary mode* over *ignited* and *infundibuliform* over *funnel-shaped*?

Needless complexity is the hallmark of a bad writer. When the big words slither into the sentence, simplicity takes wing. In writing, simplicity is the chief good; when writing is simple, it is easy to understand. It will not be simplistic unless the writer has failed to think things through. *Simplistic* describes oversimplified thought, not the expression of thought. When one ignores the complexity inherent in an event, fails to anticipate and answer the reader's questions, or disregards the reader's probable objections, then the thinking is simplistic. No degree of simplicity will rescue simplistic thought; no degree of needless complexity will long disguise it.

Do not complicate. This animal is not a *feline*, but a cat; this cat does not *masticate*, but chews; it does not chew its *sustenance*, but its food. Anyone who sees a cat chewing its food and actually thinks, "There is a sustenance-masticating feline" should be excused from writing in business; there is no hope for him.

⑨ In business, readers are ferociously impatient.

Their impatience is practical and stems from a series of expectations about business writing. The writer must understand and accept these expectations so that he can work to fulfill them.

When we read something for pleasure (a novel, feature article, or letter from an old friend), we expect a storytelling sort of presentation, a rambling journey through ideas. We demand to be kept in suspense by a good mystery story; we don't care whether our friend's letter contains a bottom-line point. But we read such documents because we choose to read them. Because we choose to read them, we disregard wordiness, lack of focus, personal quirks of style, and even errors in standard usage. The reading is relaxed and temperate.

Business documents are read with a completely different set of expectations. In business, documents receive a *functional* reading, and for this reason they must be written functionally. Keep the following ideas firmly in mind:

▪ *Readers expect you to come to the point.* Readers expect business documents to make a particular point, and they are vexed when the point is buried or (worse) never actually stated anywhere in the text. Readers of business documents expect the bottom line to be revealed in the first paragraph; if it isn't, they will certainly not behave as readers of love letters do (plucking and tasting every plum of a word and reading all the sentences in order), but they will ransack the text, rummaging impatiently until they find the point. If you begin with background or inexplicable detail, readers will skip it. They will skim until they discover what you want them to do or to know. Since this is how people read, it makes good sense to put your important ideas in the first paragraph, if not in the first sentence. Readers who hunger for background, explanation, or justification can keep reading; those uninterested in such details can stop.

■ *Readers expect economy of expression.* Descriptive writing is appropriate in a novel; wordiness is overlooked in personal letters. But the language of business documents should be as concise as you can make it. The reader is justifiably impatient with *on two separate and distinct occasions*, when all the writer means is "twice"; the reader is right to snort with exasperation when he must hack his way through *performed a thorough and complete investigation of*. He could have leapt nimbly over *thoroughly investigated*.

■ *Readers expect you to use words they understand.* If you're reading an article for pleasure and encounter the word *quondam*, you are free either to guess at its meaning or to look it up in the dictionary. Your knowing what it means isn't crucial; you don't need to do anything or decide anything, your reputation is not at risk, and money will not change hands. But if you encounter that word in a business document, you have no choice but to interrupt the reading and grab the dictionary (in business, guessing can be very expensive). Readers of business documents should never be obliged to look a word up! *Nunc pro tunc* may seem like a ripsnorting way to say *retroactively*, but a *nunc pro tunc* on a page to be read by anyone other than attorneys and scholars is the footprint of a bonehead. And it is chronic boneheadedness to insist that difficult words and phrases are appropriate merely because they happen to exist in some dictionary. The purpose of a memo is to convey something, not to mystify or impress. The bonehead writes *apposite* to prove he was there; the good writer writes *appropriate* and leaves no trace of himself.

■ *Readers expect you to conform to standard English.* When people notice errors in the writing, they stop reading and begin to edit. A reader who encounters a misspelled word, a word used in the wrong way (such as *imply* when the sense is *infer*), a semicolon when a comma is required, or any other elementary error will cease seeing your ideas and begin scrutinizing the mechanics of language. This is not what reading should be. Let no quirk, flourish, error, or awkwardness distract from the ideas themselves. In business writing, good style is the absence of "style."

☒ **Good writing sounds like good speech.**

"Good" speech is the key. Good speech communicates, with a minimum of fuss and bother, what the speaker intends; thus, a reasonable person keeps her speech simple. Only someone recently released from the asylum of business school would actually say,

> Our new advertising campaign will systematize positive corporate product image consolidation in the potential targeted customer base.

Mercifully, very few people actually hear such words come out when they open their mouths. Very few people think in such a monstrous manner. Why, then, do we read such writing? We read it because people believe that writing must differ from speech. They are right about that, but they are wrong about the nature of the difference: Writing should not be more "elevated" or "elegant" than good speech. It should simply be more precise.

But let's not leap from an airy height into muck. The oft-given instruction "Write the way you speak" is hardly the panacea. Taken on face value (which is how most people take things), "Write the way you speak" invites chaos. Unlike the listener, the reader has no access to the inflections of the voice; unless the writer puts words in the right order and punctuates appropriately, nuance and emphasis are lost. Unlike the speaker, the writer isn't present at the moment of communication and cannot react to an eyebrow raised in confusion. Writers must be far more deliberate than speakers. Furthermore, speaking is a much more relaxed activity than writing is, and most speakers, even highly educated ones, are often imprecise. A reasonable person might say, for example,

> In light of the fact that we only heard about the incident yesterday, we'll need more time to do an investigation.

Grammar here is fine, and the thought is fairly clear. The sentence suffers from the minor problems of wordiness and loose emphasis. If someone spoke that sentence, the listener would hear how *only* modifies *yesterday*, but the reader doesn't hear the writer's inflection. For this reason, writers should put words in precise order. Note, in the revision below, that the writer uses the same conversational English words; he merely places them exactly where they should go and simplifies wherever he can.

> Because we heard about the incident only yesterday, we need more time to investigate.

⑪ **Style must vary.**

Don't confuse "style" with "professional tradition." There are good reasons why scientific reports need to be dispassionate and objective, good reasons why contracts and other legal documents need to be impersonal, good reasons why proposals need to contain technical terms. In a scientific report, *It was demonstrated that gravity excludes extraneous electrons* is a perfectly fine sentence if what did the demonstrating is either obvious or irrelevant. In a legal brief, tradition justifies such sentences as *Plaintiff contends, pursuant to 24 US 311, that said affidavit is invalid.* In a technical proposal, *The AVM enables the COTA to oscillate at 600 rps* is appropriate, so long as the intended reader is familiar with the abbreviations.

What's important to understand is that readers of scientific documents expect an "objective" approach, judges expect legal "terms of art," and contracting officers expect technical detail. In every profession, traditions evolve—traditions regarding point of view, word choice, format, and so on—and these traditions establish the accepted idiom (or stylistic preferences) of a profession. When writing to members of a particular profession, writers are free to use the idiom of that profession. Since the tradition is what readers expect, arbitrarily deviating from it can backfire—not only can the deviation distract, but it can also provoke readers to wonder about the writer's expertise (and thus his credibility).

But there is a difference between conforming to a tradition simply because it is a tradition and conforming to it because it is a sensible and useful one. We must wonder whether the judge who expects *the aforesaid appeal herein* truly prefers to read such language or whether he feels doomed to read it. My guess is the latter. My guess is that readers of scientific documents feel obliged—fated—to slog through *current genetic reconfiguration methodologies*, and would tell you, if you asked them and they were honest, that they would rather read about *current methods for modifying genes.*

The jargon of law, the compact syntax of science, the abbreviations of engineers—while these may contribute to precision after two or three readings, they are difficult enough for the readers who expect them. (We can call these readers sacred, because they belong to a particular priesthood.) Clearly, when these idiomatic traditions escape their professions and encounter secular readers (i.e., those uninitiated in the mysteries), communication abruptly stops. When a customer inquires about a problem with her telephone service, such a response as *The outdial blockage consequented from a digital switching relay malfunction in the trunkline at T2* may as well be the yodelings of a Siberian husky.

Adjust your style to accommodate the reader and the occasion. Precision does not matter if it is expressed in a language foreign to the reader, and a memo thanking paralegals for contributing to a charity does not need to be written in the formidable lingo of a Memorandum Opinion and Order. The *It was thought that* and *It was observed that* of science have no place in a letter to a customer, and mysterious remarks like *EATU* (European/Asian Trafficking Unit) and *TDMA* (Time-Deferred Multiple Access) must be confined within the temple walls. Use sacred language when you converse with priests, but when you have a secular or general audience, relax the formal idiom of your profession. One wearing a tuxedo while tossing a Frisbee to his dog might make an interesting spectacle in a television commercial, but in the practical world that person would be carefully watched.

PART TWO

Techniques for Conciseness and Emphasis

On Being Concise

What *Concise* Means

Of all the myths about writing, the one that provokes the most mischief is that *Be concise* means "Be brief." Conciseness and brevity are hardly the same thing, and writers who confuse the two create cryptic, impenetrable, or ambiguous expressions.

> We need to modernize our obsolete nuclear weapons tracking system.

We're guessing if we think we know what's obsolete in that simple sentence. No hyphen alerts us to whether certain words form a unit; *obsolete* could relate to *weapons* or to *system*. If we read by the code of ordinary syntax, we'd assume that the writer means,

> We need to modernize our obsolete system for tracking nuclear weapons.

Unfortunately, the writer intends to convey something quite different:

> We need to modernize our system that tracks obsolete nuclear weapons.

The clear expression of the thought requires six words, not five. If an expression isn't clear on the first reading, then the fact that it's presented in five words (as opposed to six) is beside the point. If six or seven or a dozen words are required to convey an idea, then that is the number of words the writer should use. Conciseness demands not that we minimize the number of words in a sentence, but that we make every word count.

What Conciseness Requires

At its heart, being concise requires that writers (1) know the meanings of words, (2) choose precise words, (3) let definitions do the job, (4) remember what the reader already knows, and (5) be willing to tell the plain truth. All wordiness proceeds from the writer's disregarding one or more of these issues.

If we know the meaning of *postpone*, we would never write *put off until a later time*; if we know the meaning of *twice*, we would not write *on two separate and distinct occasions*. If we choose precisely, we write that an event *jeopardizes* a project, not that the event *negatively affects the potential success of* the project; we would write that a remark *bewildered* an audience, not that it *had the effect of leaving the audience in a very confused state*. If we respect definitions, we write of our experience and of the forecast, not of our *past experience* and of the *forecast for the future*. If the reader already knows, because the writer has already said so, that a report presents the results of the Consumer Confidence Poll of July 1993, then repeating *the July 1993 Consumer Confidence Poll report* is wordiness in the extreme. The word *report* would suffice.

Finally, if the writer has a thing to say, she should say it. If the truth of the matter is "Because of the cost overruns, I decided to cancel the contract," then *Due to the ongoing nature of the contractor's billings exceeding the terms provided in the contract, the decision to terminate the contract was made* is worse than merely wordy. It borders on deception.

Good faith. Two little words, but how important. With good faith, you need only practice technique, and conciseness will follow. Without good faith—here, *the attempt to communicate honestly*—no degree of technical skill with language will make the slightest difference.

Here are techniques that will make your writing concise. Examples are given to illustrate the techniques; in general, the examples in the column on the left are wordy and inexact, while the revisions on the right are succinct and precise.

① **Write with verbs, not with nouns.**

If you write, *The species is making a return to populated areas*, you are using *return* as a noun. Use it as a verb instead, and your writing will be much more concise: *The species is returning to populated areas*. If you write, *We gave them warning that they would have a need to create an increase in their capital reserves*, you are using *warning*, *need*, and *increase* as nouns, and the sentence is imprecise. Used as verbs, these words force precision: *We warned them that they would need to increase their capital reserves*.

Write with verbs, not with nouns. Following this instruction will make your writing clearer, more succinct, and more emphatic. When you look for a verb, ask yourself, "What, precisely, does the subject do?"

Observe the patterns in the examples below, and notice how the exact verb simplifies and invigorates the expression.

They will perform an audit of the bank next week.	They will audit the bank next week.
He made the attempt to create documentation of the problem.	He tried to document the problem.
They have made the promise to provide funding for the venture.	They have promised to fund the venture.
When we made a visit to the site, we took a tour of the missile complex.	When we visited the site, we toured the missile complex.
They performed an appraisal of the property after they did a survey of the lot.	They appraised the property after they surveyed the lot.
Our competitors are putting their reputation in jeopardy by not putting as much emphasis as they used to on customer service.	Our competitors are risking their reputation by deemphasizing customer service.
She did an analysis of the demographics and makes the claim that there will be shrinkage in our customer base.	She analyzed the demographics and claims that our customer base will shrink.
The CEO gave a speech about the importance of manifesting ethical behavior.	The CEO spoke about the importance of behaving ethically.
Readers show a preference for simplicity and do a skimming of difficult material.	Readers prefer simplicity and skim difficult material.
He gave the report that the client was exhibiting an interest in the device.	He reported that the client was interested in the device.
They did a monitoring of the site and made the discovery that the species was making a rapid recovery.	They monitored the site and discovered that the species was rapidly recovering.

② State what the subject *does*, not what it is.

Your writing will become more concise if you minimize your use of the *to be* verb (*is, am, are, be, being, been, was, were*). Instead of telling the reader what the subject is, always try to express precisely what the subject *does*. Note how emphasis improves in the following examples.

The surgeon is in vigorous opposition to the procedure.	The surgeon vigorously opposes the procedure.
The attorney's remark was very confusing to the witness.	The attorney's remark perplexed the witness.
They are still of the firm belief that the advertising is misleading to consumers.	They remain convinced that the advertising misleads consumers.
He is adamant that he was under the impression that the test was in compliance with FDA regulations.	He insists that he thought the test complied with FDA regulations.
She is the chairperson of the committee that is in oversight of the funding.	She chairs the committee that oversees funding.
This response is typical of their attitude about deadlines.	This response typifies their attitude about deadlines.
He was successful in his attempt to be persuasive to the vice president regarding the funding of the program.	He succeeded in persuading the vice president to fund the program.
Ms. Fox will be the representative of our organization at the conference.	Ms. Fox will represent us at the conference.

Use good judgment. Certainly you will sometimes need to use an *is* (and its cousins). Whenever the emphasis of the expression requires a form of the *to be* verb, use it in good faith.

> Complying with regulations *is impossible* when the regulations *are ambiguous*.

> Since the situation *is unprecedented*, we *are unsure* how to respond.

In those sentences, *is* and *are* indicate states of being; they do their job perfectly well, and it makes no sense to spend time considering how one might revise them.

③ Avoid "smothered verbs."

If you write *perform an assessment of* or *made the determination that*, you have smothered *assess* and *determined*; if you write *is in compliance with*, you have smothered *complies*. The use of nouns like *assessment* and *compliance* (which are derived from verbs) will force you into wordiness and imprecision.

Smothered verbs are simple to spot: They end in the familiar suffixes *-ion, -ment, -ance, -ence,* and *-ive.* Note the patterns of clutter in the examples on the left.

We've asked them to provide justification for the cost overrun.	We've asked them to justify the cost overrun.
The vice president gave authorization for us to make a positive adjustment to the scope of the contract.	The vice president authorized us to increase the scope of the contract.
Yesterday he made the announcement that he would turn in his resignation on Friday.	Yesterday he announced that he would resign on Friday.
The attorney is of the firm opinion that the judge will grant an extension of the deadline.	The attorney expects the judge to extend the deadline.
NRC did an investigation of the accident and came to the conclusion that the company had been in violation of safety regulations.	After investigating the accident, NRC concluded that the company had violated safety regulations.
Since no one had an objection, the committee passed a resolution to provide funding for the program.	Since no one objected, the committee resolved to fund the program.
The two satellites will have a collision unless we make an adjustment to their flight paths.	The two satellites will collide unless we adjust their flight paths.
The arbiter made recommendations on ways to effect a solution to the dispute.	The arbiter recommended ways to solve the dispute.
Her report made the implication that the agency failed to provide adequate regulation of the industry.	Her report implied that the agency failed to adequately regulate the industry.

Only if you are emphasizing the thing itself—the *solution,* for example—does it makes sense to write, *Her solution was brilliant* or *The solution satisfied everyone.* It is better to say, *His opinion is* than *He opines;* but if you intend to indicate what he *does,* then it is best to say, *He believes.* Write with everyday verbs.

④ **Challenge *make, do, give, have, provide,* and *perform.***

Challenge these verbs. While they are simple, they are usually imprecise. More often than not, you mean *remarked* when you write *made the remark that* and *permit* when you write *give permission to. Remarked* and *permit* are also simple, and they have the added virtue of being precise. Notice how the six weak verbs inflate the sentences in the left column.

His response made the audience go silent.	His response silenced the audience.
She made her customers irritated because she made no attempt to respond to their concerns.	She irritated her customers because she ignored their concerns.
They made him confused when they suddenly did a shift in their line of questioning.	They confused him when they suddenly shifted their line of questioning.
The organization does research on international monetary policy.	The organization researches international monetary policy.
They did a comparison of the two nations' nuclear armaments.	They compared the two nations' nuclear armaments.
The major gave a briefing to the general and his staff.	The major briefed the general and his staff.
This device will give us the ability to perform interception of microwave transmissions.	This device will enable us to intercept microwave transmissions.
The strategy should have a significant positive effect on sales.	The strategy should stimulate sales.
The CEO had an extremely negative response to the accusation.	The CEO bristled at the accusation.
The experience should provide us with a lesson about the danger of not paying attention to the competition.	The experience should teach us the danger of disregarding the competition.
We have asked them to provide clarification and explanation of the law.	We have asked them to clarify and explain the law.
We need to perform a periodic review of the results.	We need to review the results periodically.

⑤ **Never use *effect* and *impact* as verbs; use *affect* only in the sense of "to influence."**

Used as verbs, *effect* results in wordiness and weak emphasis, and *impact* results in ambiguity. The following sentences are "correct" English:

> This will enable us to effect a reduction in your premium.
>
> The company claims that the drug will effect a lengthening of life.
>
> The new policy will impact morale. [*How?*]
>
> If we reduce our advertising, revenue will be impacted. [*How?*]

These are correct, but they are imprecise and vague. The first two are terribly cluttered; the second two are Rorschach-inkblot sentences, begging the reader to supply a meaning. Sentences that use *impact* or *effect* as verbs are never concise or clear; they are merely "correct." If the writer wishes to emphasize something, he does it with the precise verb:

> This will enable us to reduce your premium.
>
> The company claims that the drug will prolong life.
>
> The policy will boost morale.
>
> If we reduce our advertising, revenue will decrease.

Semireasonable writers know that *impact* is vague. They admit as much when they supply adverbs, giving us such constructions as *positively impact* and *negatively impact*. The adverbs help, but the right verb would do the job much more precisely:

Simplicity of expression positively impacts clarity.	Simplicity of expression improves clarity.
The news coverage negatively impacted his reputation.	The news coverage ruined his reputation.

Like *impact*, *affect* can result in ambiguity. Consider the following sentences:

> The new regulation will certainly affect our reporting. [*How?*]
>
> The prolonged drought affected the crop. [*How?*]
>
> The launch was affected by the malfunction. [*How?*]

The reader reads what the writer writes. Presented with *affect*, the reader reads *affect*. If the writer intends to convey that reporting will be complicated, that the crop was stunted, and that the launch was delayed, then clearly those are the right words. *Delayed*, after all, is the word for *delayed*; no other word is.

Affect is the right word only when you wish to specify no particular effect. Use it as a synonym for *influence*:

> A number of variables affect the outcome.
>
> The new tax law does not affect your take-home pay.
>
> Sales have been unaffected by the news.
>
> Any change of words affects the meaning of a sentence.

6 **Challenge adverbs.**

Adverbs are often unnecessary and should always be challenged. If you write *proceeded very slowly*, challenge the *very slowly*. Would *crept* convey the idea more precisely? When you write *look closely at*, chances are good that you mean "scrutinize"; if you write *decline precipitously*, you probably mean "plunge."

Find the one-word verb that captures your meaning. Note the precision, vigor, and emphasis that this technique creates in the examples on the right.

The shareholders responded negatively to the proposal.	The shareholders rejected the proposal.
The shareholders reacted enthusiastically to the decision.	The shareholders applauded the decision.
The board of directors thought carefully about the merger.	The board of directors deliberated the merger.
The consultant spoke indistinctly as he went quickly through the material.	The consultant mumbled as he hurried through the material.
The reasons for the decline will be clearly presented in the report.	The reasons for the decline will be stated in the report.
Economists claim that the GNP is growing negatively at a 2 percent rate.	Economists claim that the GNP is shrinking at a 2 percent rate.
Economists' statements are often nearly impossible to understand.	Economists' statements frequently defy comprehension.

After she looked quickly at the report, she walked angrily from the office.	After she glanced at the report, she stormed from the office.
The consensus quickly fell apart when the news came.	The consensus collapsed when the news came.
Our employees' morale is slowly being eaten away by the litigation.	Our employees' morale is being eroded by the litigation.
This report indicates that the infrastructure is slowly losing its integrity.	This report indicates that the infrastructure is disintegrating.

⑦ **Reveal the verb early.**

The right verb confers precision and emphasis; introducing it early in the sentence will make the writing efficient and instantly clear. Pick the word you intend to use as the subject—and then don't dawdle. Put a precise verb right beside it. The following sentence typifies what will happen if you don't:

> The measure and breadth of our activities to prevent and to remedy tropical deforestation, especially in Equatorial South America, where the rain forest is being depleted at the rate of 1,000 acres each week, follow.

The reader hungers for the verb. The writer knows what the subject is doing. The reader does not. She holds her breath until the verb arrives, because until it arrives she has no sense of what the overall expression is about. And in sentences like the one above, the reader is gasping for breath. Try not to separate the verb from the subject; put those words as close together as you can. Note how clarity improves in the sentences on the right.

It may be that a very good and sensible reason for their refusal to reveal the information we have requested exists.	They may have reason for refusing to reveal the information.
That the software, despite its cost and the time it takes to master, will be ultimately beneficial is probable.	We will probably benefit from the software, despite its cost and the time required to master it.

According to the survey, drug-abuse counseling programs by more than half of the *Fortune* 500 companies in the 1980s were instituted.	The survey reveals that drug-abuse counseling programs were instituted by more than half of the *Fortune* 500 companies in the 1980s.
The lobbyist's behavior in this matter of promising the senator a campaign contribution of $100,000 in return for his vote to increase farm subsidies is clearly illegal.	The lobbyist clearly broke the law by promising the senator a $100,000 campaign contribution in return for his vote to increase farm subsidies.
Your proposal to provide consulting services to help this organization streamline paperflow, expedite the writing process, and improve customer correspondence in this organization is accepted.	We accept your proposal to help us streamline paperflow, expedite the writing process, and improve customer correspondence.
Approval by the committee of the bill that would illegitimize all automatic and semiautomatic weapons from importation into the United States is strongly anticipated.	We expect the committee to approve the bill that would outlaw importing automatic and semiautomatic weapons.

8   Don't worry about "passive" or "active"; just put the right word first and tell the truth.

Many people blame the passive voice for most of the ills in business writing. To do so is to generalize in the worst way. The passive is frequently necessary, and writers who believe it is "bad" or "weak" will often emphasize the wrong idea.

Let's make very certain that we understand what we're talking about. A sentence is said to be active when the subject acts; it is said to be passive when the subject receives the action.

Active	*Passive*
The Redskins beat the Eagles.	The Eagles were beaten by the Redskins.
We received the imagery analysis today.	The imagery analysis was received today.

If we ask which of those are better sentences, we have asked a meaningless question. All are fine. All are simple, emphatic, and free of clutter. The active sentences emphasize the Redskins and the *we*; the passive sentences emphasize the Eagles and the imagery analysis. The question with teeth is this: What do you intend to emphasize? What are you going to talk about in the sentences that follow? Emphasis should determine which word you use as the subject of the sentence. Once you've decided what to emphasize, all you need to do is tell the truth. The following sentences are perfectly reasonable.

The issue was not decided by the committee.	*Passive; emphasizes* issue, *and the writer will go on to discuss the issue.*
The committee adjourned before deciding the issue.	*Active; emphasizes* committee, *and the writer will go on to discuss the committee.*
Writers should use the passive voice in good faith.	*Active; emphasizes* writers, *and the writer will go on to discuss writers.*
The passive voice should be used in good faith.	*Passive; emphasizes the* passive voice, *and the writer will go on to discuss the passive.*

Few adults actually write such awkward-sounding sentences as *Your remarks are appreciated by me* or *The report was written by me*. When you see an expression like that, the fault lies not with the passive construction but with the assumption that has produced the construction: Somewhere along the line, the writer was told very forcefully that he must never, ever use *I* in formal writing.

The sentences below are passive and are perfectly clear.

We were flabbergasted by the results.	*Stresses how we were affected.*
The audit will be completed next week.	*Stresses the audit, not the auditors.*
These questions are ambiguously phrased.	*Who wrote the questions is irrelevant.*
The mistakes have been corrected.	*Who corrected the mistakes is irrelevant.*
Their objection was unexpected.	*Who failed to expect it is obvious.*

The passive voice can contribute to poor writing, but blaming it for sentences such as the ones below is like blaming the airwaves for nonsense on television. The fault lies with the originating mind, who gets the logic backwards.

Reading this document is forbidden by those persons without "Top Secret" clearance.	*Persons without "Top Secret" clearance are doing the forbidding?*

The handling of laboratory animals is strictly prohibited by unauthorized personnel.	*The unauthorized personnel are prohibiting others?*
Legislation is being considered to reduce the COLA in the House of Representatives.	*The House is considering reducing its own cost-of-living adjustment?*

The following sentences in the left column may be passive, but wild syntax and big words are what interfere with clarity. Converting them to the active voice helps, but simpler words help more.

It was demonstrated that the effect of elevated temperature on the compound was negligible by this experiment.	This experiment demonstrated that increased heat has little effect on the compound.
That she was accosted by the D Section lamppost in the parking lot is alleged and maintained by the complainant.	The complainant states that she was accosted near the D Section lamppost in the parking lot.
There were no apparent reasons why the determination was made by EPA of endangered species classification in the report.	The report failed to indicate why EPA has classified the species as "endangered."

The sentence in the left column here is passive, but the main difficulty with it is its length. A good writer never makes a reader work so hard.

The failure to report the overrun within the time specified by the contract and according to procedures therein was attributed to a new project manager's being uncertain about the requirements by OSI.	According to OSI, the overrun was not reported promptly because the new project manager was unaware of the requirement to do so.

Don't despise the passive voice. Use it when emphasis and context demand its use. It is senseless to try to make every sentence active; when you do that, you alter emphasis.

Active:	The Redskins beat the Eagles. [*Credits the Redskins.*]
Passive:	The Eagles were beaten by the Redskins. [*Emphasizes the Eagles but credits the Redskins.*]
Active:	The Eagles lost to the Redskins. [*Does not credit the Redskins.*]

⑨ **Challenge *it is* and *there are* constructions.**

Precise writing emphasizes a precise subject. *It is* and *There are* dilute emphasis and usually waste the reader's time. Smokescreen expressions such as *It was discovered that* and *There were insinuations made to the effect that* are the constructions that have ruined the reputation of the passive voice. A good writer minimizes his use of them.

Which of the sentences below better emphasizes the idea?

It was believed by the defense that it was likely that the jury would not be able to reach a verdict.

The defense believed that the jury would probably fail to reach a verdict.

There are indications given by the test that there are a number of errors still left in the program.

The test indicates that errors remain in the program.

The good writer comes to the point. *It* and *there* are rarely the point, and the deliberate writer emphasizes the word that is.

It is recommended by the investment bank that we pursue the acquisition.

The investment bank recommends that we pursue the acquisition.

It is the opinion of this office that it would be best if the contract were to be canceled without undue delay.

We believe that the contract should be canceled now.

It is clearly specified in the Code of Ethics that there is no excuse for accepting favors from contractors.

The Code of Ethics clearly prohibits accepting favors from contractors.

There would seem to be no way to overcome the conflict.

The conflict appears insurmountable.

Use these constructions only when not using them would result in even more complicated sentences. Employing them in the sentences in the right column enables the writer to improve clarity by revealing the verb early in the sentence.

Holding that the passive voice is to be avoided at all costs does not make sense.

It makes no sense to hold that the passive voice is to be avoided at all costs.

Demanding that the auditors revise their findings is unethical.

It is unethical to demand that the auditors revise their findings.

⑩ **Have a very good reason when you conceal the actor.**

Below are examples of the construction called the divine passive (it's called that because only the Divinity knows who the actor is).

It was decided to abort the launch.

Mistakes were made.

Unfortunately, a serious error was committed in the calculation.

Unlike the ordinary passive voice, such sentences do not reveal the actor; none identifies the decider, maker, or committer. Is this construction sensible? Is it bad? That depends.

It was decided to abort the launch, which skirts the issue of who decided, might be a perfectly reasonable sentence. Omitting the actor is reasonable if certain things are true:

- Only the fact of the decision is pertinent; who decided is irrelevant.
- The writer does not know and therefore cannot say precisely who was responsible for the decision.
- Context vigorously implies who made the decision.

In everyday English, the construction is used all the time. It was used in the sentence you just read, and it's being used in this one as well. In expressions such as *It's supposed to rain tomorrow* and *The animal was believed to be extinct*, the actors are either implied or irrelevant. In ordinary style, no one says, *Meteorologists suppose that rain will fall tomorrow* and *The animal was believed by biologists to be extinct*. Context implies those things.

On the other hand, if the writer of *It was decided to abort the launch* is using the construction merely to avoid taking responsibility for an action—to avoid admitting that he, Dr. Eisenreich, or Colonel Kirk made what turned out to be a bad decision—then we have landed with a resounding *plop!* in the thick soup of bad faith. It is at this point that questions of style and usage go out the window. One reluctant to take responsibility—in this case, to confess—will find the divine passive an extremely useful construction.

If the identity of the actor is important and would not otherwise be apparent, the honest writer reveals it, as in the right column:

It is recommended that the contract be awarded to CCI.	I recommend awarding the contract to CCI.

| The decision was made not to proceed with the research. | We decided to end the research. |

⑪ Find the word that captures the sense.

Some people believe that a lengthy expression better emphasizes an idea than a brief expression does. Paradoxically, the opposite is true: *Fire!* bursts into the mind far more readily than does *For reasons of an incipient incendiary event, it is strongly recommended that immediate evacuation of the premises be undertaken.*

Length dilutes; brevity emphasizes. Needless words dilute emphasis in precisely the same way that too much water weakens tea.

A halt to the ongoing exceeding of the contract by the costs associated with the program is absolutely imperative.	The overruns must stop.
In close proximity to Mount St. Helens, seismic tremors have begun to occur at thirty-second intervals of time.	Near Mount St. Helens, tremors now occur every thirty seconds.
Our experience in the past gives the strong indication that adding additional incentives seldom if ever has the result of convincing customers to purchase automotive units.	Our experience strongly indicates that added incentives seldom induce customers to buy cars.

When the writer finds the right word, she doesn't need a lot of almost-right ones to make her point. When we write *from time to time* or *once in awhile*, we mean "occasionally"; when we write *as a general rule*, we mean "usually" or "generally." Don't define the word in the sentence.

The police are now of the suspicion that the fire was intentionally set.	The police now suspect arson.
His argument went here and there and all over the place, apparently without a goal.	His argument wandered aimlessly.
It is our conclusion that a spark caused the boxes to burst into flame.	We conclude that a spark ignited the boxes.

She embodies an example of a good manager.	She exemplifies good management.
The clause contains several plausible interpretations.	The clause is ambiguous.
Employees must on an interim basis use the lounge on the third floor.	Employees must temporarily use the lounge on the third floor.

Think with individual words, not with phrases. Fitting the flesh of words onto the spirit of ideas is an activity as mysterious as conjuring, and each of us is a sorcerer. But what would we think of a sorcerer who tried to conjure a hummingbird and called up a hippo instead? We would see a fat walloping hippo, and the sorcerer's insistence that he *meant* a hummingbird would not change what we see. Avoid the packaged phrases. The lumbering expressions below all mean "because":

    in light of the fact that
    in view of the fact that
    in consideration of the fact that
    because of the fact that
    due to the fact that
    given the fact that
    for the reason that
    inasmuch as
    on account of
    on the grounds that
    owing to the fact that

Indiscriminately spewing the first words that come to mind is a good idea when you are drafting the document. When you revise, discriminate: Replace the spewed phrase with a precise word. Notice the improvement in the sentences on the right.

Owing to the fact that Colonel Senchak has diplomatic immunity, conducting a prosecution of him is well outside the realm of possibility.	Because Colonel Senchak has diplomatic immunity, prosecuting him is impossible.
Dr. Wells was interrupted only on one distinct occasion, but the interruption lasted for a thirty-minute period of time.	Dr. Wells was interrupted only once, but the interruption lasted thirty minutes.
She has on numerous occasions made the attempt to provide reasons for her decision.	She has often tried to explain her decision.

We are making the request that you provide payment in a timely manner.

We ask that you pay promptly.

We tried on two separate occasions to bring the variables to a minimum.

We tried twice to minimize the variables.

We are at this point in time of the opinion that gravity waves are the reason for the disturbance.

We currently believe that gravity waves cause the disturbance.

In the final analysis, good writing is a reflection of an honest mind.

Ultimately, good writing reflects honesty.

Beginning this year and continuing indefinitely into the future, distribution of dividends will be made on an annual basis.

From now on, dividends will be paid annually.

Despite the fact that he is, as a general rule, hard to pin down precisely, Senator Karp on this occasion gave a complete, precise, and thorough response to the question that was put to him.

Although he is usually evasive, Senator Karp answered the question thoroughly and precisely.

The vice president made the request that we abbreviate the presentation to make it less time-consuming.

The vice president asked us to shorten the presentation.

The software costs the sum of $4,000, but due to the fact that it will make it simpler for us to keep track of indirect costs, it is my opinion that the purchase of it is practical.

The software costs $4,000, but because it will simplify our tracking indirect costs, I believe we should buy it.

At this moment in time, in the absence of a sufficient amount of data, we can only provide an approximation of the results.

Currently, without enough data, we can only approximate the results.

Despite the fact that the study team did not bother to do an analysis of the soil, the results give a fairly clear indication that the residue of uranium is present.

Although the study team neglected to analyze the soil, the results clearly indicate uranium residue.

The CEO gave a speech in a short span of time regarding the dutiful obligation a company has to the individuals who own shares of stock in it.

The CEO spoke briefly about a company's obligation to its shareholders.

In the event that the elevators are dysfunctional, proceed with an immediate contact of Building Maintenance.	If the elevators are not working, call Building Maintenance immediately.

Do not be brief at the expense of tone. Whenever establishing a friendly and personal tone is as important as the message, then longer and more conversational phrases are appropriate. In a memo whose purpose is to thank employees for an extraordinary effort, for example, a CEO might write, *I'd like to express my deepest appreciation for the long hours you've recently put in* rather than *Thank you for working overtime* or *Your dedication gratifies me.* These two are succinct but fail to convey any genuine sense of gratitude; because they are dispassionate, they preserve an impersonal separation between the writer and his readers. Maintaining that the longer sentence is "wordy" is a failure to understand both the purpose of such a statement and the nature of authentic communication—it is tantamount to arguing that music should be concise.

⑫ Beware *basis, manner,* and *way.*

When they come at the end of prepositional phrases, *basis, manner, way,* and *fashion* nearly always signal wordiness. In ordinary (relaxed) conversation, people speak quite naturally about a situation developing *in a rapid manner* and an activity being done *on a spontaneous basis.* Writing should be much more precise.

Challenge these words each time you use them. Sometimes they are unavoidable, as in *They responded in a friendly way* or *The defendant muttered in an ugly way.* (These certainly sound more like English than *They responded friendlily* and *The defendant muttered uglily.*) Note the patterns; all you need to do is salvage the precise adverb or verb.

The phrase:	*means:*
in a timely manner	promptly, soon
in a predictable manner	predictably
on an annual basis	annually, each year
on an interim basis	temporarily
found A in an accidental way	discovered A
B fell in a precipitous way	B plummeted
C spoke in a muffled fashion	C murmured
leave X in a secure fashion	secure X

Phrases involving *basis, manner, way,* and *fashion* inflate the sentences in the left column. Note how conciseness improves in the sentences on the right.

All redundant systems must be checked on a routine basis.	All redundant systems must be routinely checked.
The maintenance was performed in a hit-or-miss way.	The maintenance was performed haphazardly.
The satellite is behaving in a unique and peculiar manner.	The satellite is behaving strangely.
They respond to customers' complaints in a timely fashion and in a courteous manner.	They respond promptly and courteously to customers' complaints.
The waste site must be watched in a careful way on an ongoing basis.	The waste site must be monitored continuously.
We need to respond in a firm manner but in a discreet fashion.	We need to respond firmly but discreetly.
A good writer will speak his truth in an honest way and in a simple manner.	A good writer will speak his truth honestly and simply.

13 Be alert to "intruders."

"Intruders" are nouns that have nothing in particular to do and decide to crash the party. In a sentence such as *The deficit conditions are worsening*, the word *conditions* is an intruder. In plain style, what is worsening is the deficit, and the writer should say so: *The deficit is worsening*. Other common intruders include *activity, program, effort, project,* and *situation*.

The reader reads what the writer writes—and when we write something like *Our college recruiting program was very successful*, the reader must assume that we are talking not about the recruiting, but about the program. If we do intend to discuss the overall program, then that is a fine sentence. But if we want the reader to understand that the *recruiting* was the successful thing, then the word *program* is deceptive. When we want to emphasize a thing, we use it not as an adjective, but as a noun: *Our college recruiting was very successful*. Just ask yourself which word you intend to emphasize.

Below, in the sentences on the left, note how each intruding word claims attention for itself, always at the expense of the word deserving emphasis.

Managers are alarmed at the deteriorating sales situation.	Managers are alarmed by the deteriorating sales.
The launch was postponed because of high wind conditions.	The launch was postponed because of high winds.

The construction effort is on schedule.	The construction is on schedule.
The consultant suggested several ways to simplify our marketing activities.	The consultant suggested several ways to simplify our marketing.
He said that the training program was helpful.	He said that the training was helpful.
The lack of on-site operatives continues to compromise our intelligence-gathering effort.	The lack of on-site operatives continues to compromise our intelligence gathering.
A better diplomatic effort would decrease the hostile conditions between the countries.	Better diplomacy would reduce the hostility between the two countries.
Responsive customer service activities are an essential condition for any business.	Responsive customer service is essential to any business.
A necessary activity for any socially conscious organization is a paper-recycling program.	All socially conscious organizations recycle paper.
Stable climatic conditions are crucial to our genetically engineered tomatoes program.	A stable climate is crucial for our genetically engineered tomatoes.
After the thorough research initiative, we were able to pinpoint the software error problems.	After thorough research, we identified the software errors.
Pay attention to details in your written communication.	Attend to details in your writing.

14 Avoid redundancy.

Remember the meanings of words. Because *history*, by definition, concerns only the past, the phrase *past history* is redundant; because *November* is a month, *the month of November* is redundant. In *Advance planning will enable us to completely avoid hidden pitfalls*, the writer is ignoring the definitions of *planning*, *avoid*, and *pitfall*. Don't say things that go without saying. Explicitly stating the implied words dilutes emphasis, complicates reading, wrecks the writer's credibility, and often misleads.

Ordinary speech teems with redundant expressions; their sheer familiarity seduces us into accepting them without question. But each time we read that someone wore a smile *on her face*, that someone has taken a leave *of absence*, or that someone has plans *for the future*, we are observing the vapor trail of a mind on autopilot. For those alert to redundancy, life is a never-ending journey through Wonderland, as signs declare, *This gate is locked to prevent entry* and *Unwanted trespassers will be prosecuted by the law.* When the guard comes to sort out the unwanted from the wanted trespassers, he is a *security guard*, and he does not merely arrive but *arrives on the scene*, and he does not arrive at midnight, but at *twelve o'clock midnight.*

Respect definitions and let them do the work. Avoid such overlapping meanings as *specific example, advance warning, past experience, carefully scrutinize, postpone until later, completely destroyed,* and *whether or not.* Remember the understanding that the reader brings to the page, and cut every word that does not further understanding.

How to Test for Redundancy

Whether an expression is redundant depends on what the reader knows. What degree of expertise does the reader bring to the page? Does the reader know that 1993 is a year? If so, then such a phrase as *in the year 1993* is redundant, and *in 1993* will suffice. Does the reader know that when people nod, they nod *their heads in agreement* and when they shrug, they shrug *their shoulders?* If so, then *nod* and *shrug* will do. Every professional knows what an island is, so to point out that Mangareva is an island *entirely surrounded on all sides by water* is to add a flurry of syllables that melt before they add anything helpful.

Silly redundancies (7 A.M. *in the morning, including but not limited to,* and *a period of three weeks*) are easy to spot; all we need to do is remember definitions. But often the matter is far more subtle, and the writer must use discretion.

Consider the following sentence:

Venezuela, a South American country, is a member of OPEC.

Is the phrase *a South American country* redundant? For some readers, it is; for other readers, it provides useful information. Arguing that people should know where Venezuela is gets the writer nowhere. If the reader doesn't know that Venezuela is in South America, then he doesn't know that Venezuela is in South America, and no degree of wishful thinking or academic bellyaching will change that. The practical question is this: Does the precise emphasis of my sentence depend on the reader's being reminded that Venezuela is in South America? Do most readers believe that OPEC consists entirely of countries in the Middle East? If so, then *a South American country* is a useful phrase.

Consider the following sentence:

The onlookers were horrified when the space shuttle *Challenger* exploded.

Is the phrase *the space shuttle* redundant? That depends on what the reader knows. If all readers know that *Challenger* was a space shuttle, then the phrase is unnecessary and should be cut; if some readers don't know that *Challenger* was a space shuttle, and the writer's meaning depends on their knowing it, then the phrase is essential. Things that "go without saying" for some readers need to be said for other readers. Remember your audience's degree of expertise.

With the reader's expertise in mind, writers can avoid redundancy by (1) knowing the meaning of words and (2) asking this question: as opposed to? In *Additional financial funding is absolutely essential for the end completion of the project*, the writer who knows the meaning of *funding* should inquire of his adjective, "*Financial? As opposed to some other kind of funding?*" He should do this twice more in his sentence, looking at the meaning of *essential* and *completion* and challenging *absolutely* and *end*. In plain style, his meaning is concisely expressed as *Additional funding is essential for the completion of this project*.

Some redundant expressions send the mind lurching off into the realm of science fiction. *She is pregnant with a baby* and *Tattoos While U Wait* beg the questions of what else she might be pregnant with and whether U could ever leave an arm or a buttock behind, have it tattooed, and pick it up later. *With a baby*—as opposed to? *While U Wait*—as opposed to?

The Right Motive, the Wrong Technique

Writers sometimes commit redundancies from an honest motive— that of clarifying a word they believe their readers may not know. While this is decent behavior, it results from a misstep in word choice; explanations and clarifications will be unnecessary if the writer chooses words well in the first place.

Take, for example, the phrase *consensus of opinion*. One who writes this redundancy evidently believes that his readers don't know what *consensus* means. But if readers are unfamiliar with *consensus*, wouldn't it make more sense to respect the meanings of words and write *shared opinion*? After all, the purpose of the sentence isn't to expand the reader's vocabulary but merely to make a point.

If readers aren't familiar with a particular word, then it's best to use a different word. One who writes, *He fell and broke the humerus bone in his left arm* must assume that his readers don't know what a "humerus" is.

(It is always a bone and always in the arm.) Readers who don't know what a humerus is may be edified to learn that it is a bone, but they still do not know which arm-bone it is and, more to the point, increasing their vocabulary is not the goal of the sentence. *He fell and broke his left arm* would be tidy if that is all the writer means. If the precise location of the injury is important, then *He fell and broke his left arm between the elbow and the shoulder* would perform admirably. Readers do not need to encounter a "humerus" in order to get on with understanding.

Avoid redundant explanations of difficult words. Pick simple words in the first place. Rather than write the profoundly redundant *She experienced a sudden cardiac infarction of the heart*, it is better to say *She had a heart attack*; rather than write about *herbivorous dinosaurs that ate plants*, it is better to write about *plant-eating dinosaurs*.

Illogical Emphasis

In his excitement, the fighter pilot radios that the target was *totally destroyed*; in the heat of her impassioned speech, the politician declares that a bill would impose a *difficult hardship* on an industry. No one would argue that *totally destroyed* is unemphatic—but it is redundant, and *obliterated* captures the meaning in a word. In the same vein, *difficult* does promote the idea of hardship—but *difficult hardship* is redundant, and *the bill would cripple the industry* is far more emphatic. In emotional moments, few people bother to be exact in their choice of words. But business writing is an activity best done with a cool head. It's best to honor the meanings of words.

Consider the STOP sign. In its succinctness, it epitomizes plain style. All it says is STOP. That's all it says because (1) that's all readers need and (2) STOP means "stop" without qualification (there are no degrees of stopping). If the sign read STOP COMPLETELY, it would be redundant; if it read STOP IN A THOROUGH MANNER BEFORE PROCEEDING, it would be absurd in its disrespect both for the meaning of words and for what the reader brings to the discourse. If it read ANY AND ALL PERSONS OPERATING A VEHICLE OF ANY DESCRIPTION FOR ANY PURPOSE WHATSOEVER ARE HEREBY ADVISED THAT A COMPLETE AND THOROUGH CESSATION OF FORWARD MOTION IS A LEGAL OBLIGATION BEFORE PROCEEDING IN AFOREMENTIONED VEHICLE THROUGH THIS INTERSECTION, it would have crashed the boundaries of the absurd, plunged down the rabbit hole, and wander goggling—with other such writing ironically called legal—in the Zone Beyond Reason.

STOP is plain style. *Stop* means "stop." Nothing else is required; anything else would not merely be unnecessary but would beg the reader to find loopholes. Even *stop completely* is silly. But such phrases as *joint agreement* and *mutual cooperation* are just as silly—if you think about them. *I love you* is a handy thing to say to a loved one; *I currently love you* will not be as well received.

Honor definitions and let them do the work. One who writes *positive growth* has forgotten that his readers know what *growth* means; one who writes *foul stench* must think his readers are unable to catch a foul whiff from *stench*. A smell can be foul or pleasant, but a *stench* is always foul and an *aroma* is always pleasant. (Does *foul aroma* sound reasonable?) When you modify a word, make sure that the modifier contributes to clarity; modify only when you wish to indicate a degree.

Some things (like damage) occur in degrees. It is sensible to write *slightly damaged* or *heavily damaged*; it is equally sensible to write *recent experience* or *driving rain*. But it is preposterous to write *past experience, falling rain, depreciate in value, collaborate together, completely totaled, entirely surrounded,* or *utterly dead*. In the following sentences, the implied words have been crossed out.

In ~~the month of~~ August ~~in the year~~ 1991, the Baltic States declared their ~~total and complete~~ independence from the Soviet Union.

Because he is ~~a qualified~~ expert in ~~the area of~~ wetlands management, we have asked ~~for~~ him to ~~assist in~~ helping us write the Environmental Impact Statement ~~document~~.

She was unsure whether ~~or not~~ to extend the ~~established~~ tradition of avoiding ~~the pronoun~~ *I* in business writing.

Throughout the ~~entire past~~ history of Western civilization, ~~certain~~ specific tenets ~~and ideas~~ have been ~~basic~~ fundamental.

Unless we base our forecast ~~for the future~~ on our ~~past~~ experience, we will prolong ~~the duration of~~ these ~~unfounded~~ rumors.

Thanks to their ~~joint~~ cooperation, the companies now enjoy many ~~positive and desirable~~ benefits.

We have decided to postpone ~~until a later time~~ adding any ~~additional confining~~ restrictions to the ESOP.

Our last invoice ~~for payment~~ has been ~~completely~~ ignored by the client, whose ~~utter~~ refusal to pay ~~funds~~ promptly ~~and in a timely manner still~~ remains ~~and continues to be~~ a serious ~~and unresolved~~ problem.

Upon ~~close~~ scrutiny, his ~~internal~~ memorandum regarding his leave ~~of absence seemed to suggest that he~~ implied that he was not given ~~adequate enough~~ time to recuperate ~~from his illness~~.

His ~~personal~~ opinion is that imports ~~from foreign countries~~ actually foster ~~positive~~ competition by American companies, but he ~~still~~

remains ~~diametrically~~ opposed to the ~~complete~~ elimination of ~~trade~~ import quotas.

15   Don't "double" terms.

Draw no distinctions where no distinctions exist. The sentence below makes sense only if (1) the thing is formally referred to as a *finding and conclusion* or (2) a *finding* differs from a *conclusion* and *the distinction is clear* in the reader's mind.

> Please send us your findings and conclusions by September 30.

If a *finding* is the same thing as a *conclusion*, then we have a "doubling" on our hands. Besides cluttering the writing, doublings wreck clarity: They mislead, as the reader believes that the ideas are distinct (when they are not).

Unless a writer is hypnotized, she will never write such a sentence as *The full scope and extent of our activities are explained in the report. Scope* and *extent* convey precisely the same meaning; no distinction is being drawn. Respect the reader's ability to supply the definitions of ordinary words, and draw no distinctions where no distinctions exist.

Notice how eliminating the doublings in the sentences below improves emphasis and clarity. Notice also that, when faced with a decision as to which word or phrase to cut, the writer cuts the one that is fancier or less precise.

> A more thoughtful ~~and considered~~ ranking ~~and ordering~~ of our long-term goals is ~~both necessary and~~ essential.
>
> The defendant contends ~~and attests~~ that he was ~~not present but~~ elsewhere ~~at the time~~ when the crime was committed.
>
> They replied ~~in response~~ that they could find few ways ~~or means~~ to distinguish ~~or differentiate~~ his proposal from the others ~~they received~~.
>
> The CEO asks ~~and requests~~ that we ~~evaluate and~~ assess the potential impact ~~and effect~~ of the information before distributing ~~or promulgating~~ it.

Some doublings, such as *betwixt and between*, are patently silly. Others, such as *if and when* and *until and unless*, fail to convey. If you have plans to do a thing, write *when*; if you have no plans but wish to introduce the possibility of doing something, write *if*. The same distinction applies for *until* and *unless*. The sentences below are clear. Doublings would cloud their meanings.

> When we convert to the new software, we will be more productive.
> If we convert to the new software, we will be more productive.

> Until OSHA adopts stricter regulations, such accidents will recur.
> Unless OSHA adopts stricter regulations, such accidents will recur.

16 **Assert.**

Use *not* only for special emphasis. *Not* frequently victimizes the reader, presenting him with ambiguity and forcing him to guess at a meaning.

> DSI does not believe that the funding should be terminated.

At first glance, readers might interpret that sentence to mean, "DSI believes that the funding should continue." *Warning*: Readers might interpret it in a hundred other ways. All the reader knows for sure is a thing DSI does *not* believe. The question, always, is what the subject *does* believe. Does DSI believe the funding should be *reduced, delayed, justified,* or possibly *scrutinized*? Or perhaps DSI does not *believe* that the funding should be terminated but actually *disputes, doubts, denies, accepts,* or even *insists*. For all any reader knows, the writer might have been attempting to say, *DSI regrets that the funding will be terminated* or *DSI believes that the funding should be monitored.*

Negations often leave the meaning very much up in the air. To control and direct the reader's understanding, a good writer *asserts*. The innocent-sounding sentence *All of the options are not practical* typifies the problem; the reader can select from a smorgasbord of meanings:

> Some of the options are impractical.
> Some of the options are practical.
> All of the options are impractical.
> None of the options is practical.

If clarity and precision matter to you, you will carefully weigh each *not*. If results are not valid, then call them *invalid*. If a decision is not acceptable, then call it *unacceptable*. The flight did not arrive on time? In plain style, it arrived either *late* or *early*. *They did not remember to* is merely a long-winded way to say *they forgot*, just as *he did not bother to* is windy for *he neglected*.

Needless to say, if one *not* can cause such confusion, does it make good sense to use two? "Two negatives equal a positive" is one of those things we accept—until we observe the language in action. Two negatives do not equal a positive; they create a mooncalf. Tell your spouse that you are "not unhappy" with your marriage and watch the response. Set theory aside; observe what truly happens. You'll have time for reflection on your way home from the florist.

If you're happy, then the right word is *happy*. If a thing is likely, avoid referring to it as *not unlikely*. If a thing is *not untrue*, a reasonably good word for it is *true*. *What is the color of a not-unwhite dog?* is a Zen-like question, enjoyable to contemplate, perhaps, but hardly a practical way of asking anything in particular. And sentences containing two or three negations often behave like thoroughly greased piglets:

> We do not now and never have maintained that the company's failure to report those assets may not have been unintentional.

When to Use *not un-* Constructions

The dishonest writer uses *not un-* constructions to avoid commitment or responsibility. He will tell you that a situation was *not unpredictable* (and leave it at that) to avoid saying that the thing was predictable and that he failed to do his job predicting it. This is yet another instance of bad faith, but it occurs so often that *not un-* has (like the innocent passive) become taboo in business writing.

Every construction in the language has its place. The honest writer (whose motto, in a nutshell, is "Do what works") uses a *not un-* construction in good faith whenever one is logically required. One is required when the writer's job is to refute the kind of contentions that sound like this:

> Detecting the missiles with infrared alone is impossible.
>
> The attorney is unlikely to file another appeal.
>
> It is unusual for the species to be seen so far north.
>
> The effects of the regulation were unforeseen.

If someone contends that a thing is *impractical*, common sense argues that the simple refutation is *not impractical*. Common sense, however, doesn't stop there. When you refute something, you are also obliged to assert something:

> Detecting the missiles with infrared alone may be very difficult, but it is not impossible.

The language of the regulation is not precise and not consistent, and therefore the meaning is not clear.	The language of the regulation is imprecise and inconsistent, and therefore the meaning is unclear.
It is not unlikely that the agency will not neglect to send another squad.	The agency will probably send another squad.
It is not unusual for them not to be in full and complete compliance with EPA regulations.	They often fail to comply completely with EPA regulations.
We are not of the belief that the software has undergone insufficient testing.	We believe that the software has been adequately tested.
This report intentionally does not include information whose source has not been verified.	This report excludes information from unverified sources.
It is not improbable that they were not unaware of the radioactive spill.	We believe they knew about the radioactive spill.
The proposal is not acceptable because it does not take our schedule into consideration.	The proposal is unacceptable because it disregards our schedule.
It is not out of the question that they will not fail to market the product before we do.	They may be able to market the product before we do.
The committee did not succeed in its attempt to make the amendment not part of the bill.	The committee failed to exclude the amendment.
The regulation does not exclude all trade with Haiti.	The regulation permits some trade with Haiti.

17 Avoid "noun strings."

The U.S. NATO counterpart forces will enjoy a constant relative combat matériel potential radio advantage vis-à-vis their Soviet counterparts during the 1990s.

—*U.S. Army Concepts Analysis Agency*

"Never use two words when one word will do" is excellent advice. But so is this: Never use one word when you need two. Writers who confuse conciseness with brevity will pile noun upon noun—a technique that lets them do away with prepositions and verbs—and the result is usually an expression that squirms and spasms in the mind.

The directorate has inferior component labeling procedures.

Four words. But what's *inferior*? To clarify that, the expression requires five words. If you mean *inferior procedures for labeling components*, write that; if you mean *procedures for labeling inferior components*, write *that*. Use as many words as clarity demands.

The writer's job is to convey—not to "be brief." Omitting useless words is always a good idea, but the operative word there is *useless*. When an expression is too brief, it will usually (1) fail to communicate or (2) convey something that the writer does not intend.

Writers beg for trouble in both regards when they express their ideas in strings of nouns. The noun that can do the work of an adjective has never been seen in the wild, but this doesn't stop some writers from breeding them in captivity. They breed like field mice. Here's a sentence that typifies the problem:

> adjective   adjective   noun   adjective   noun
> The company offers outstanding long-term employee medical benefits.

Even if we overlook the fact that this is not human speech, precisely what is *outstanding* there? To what, exactly, does *long-term* apply? Can you distinguish the possible meanings in this ambiguous construction?

> The company offers outstanding, long-term medical benefits to employees.

> The company offers outstanding medical benefits to long-term employees.

> The company offers medical benefits to outstanding, long-term employees.

"Noun strings," also called squirming nouns because the meaning refuses to sit still, can easily be simplified. Put the important word first, and then talk about it in everyday English. For example:

Rather than write:	We need an updated payroll cost analysis program.
It is clearer to write:	We need to update our program that analyzes payroll costs.
	or
	We need a program to update our analysis of payroll costs.

Rather than write:	The company received a one-year contract extension grant.
It is clearer to write:	The company received a one-year extension to the contract.

or

The company's one-year contract was extended.

In the examples below, note that the technique is consistent. Just put the important word first (changing it to a verb whenever you can). Note also that many of the revised sentences in the right column are longer than the original versions in the left column.

The Federal Reserve Board began the regulation preparation on October 1.	The Federal Reserve Board began preparing the regulation on October 1.
The task force is in the midst of paperwork reduction methods research.	The task force is researching ways to reduce paperwork.
The CEO decided that the company needed sexual harassment reporting policy changes.	The CEO decided that the company needed to change the policy for reporting sexual harassment.
NOAA scientists are currently engaged in hurricane severity prediction technique improvement.	NOAA scientists are currently improving techniques for predicting the severity of hurricanes.
She needs a copy of the competition assessment study report.	She needs a copy of the report that assesses our competition.
The vice president said he could not make sense of the audit report boilerplate language.	The vice president said he could not understand the boilerplate language in the audit report.
The experts disagree about the Stanford Medical School drug abuse report implications.	The experts disagree about the implications of Stanford Medical School's report on drug abuse.
ABA is now performing an interest rate increase impact study.	ABA is studying the effect of increased interest rates.
The completed required capital reserve analysis is due at the RTC next week.	The completed analysis of capital reserve requirements is due at the RTC next week.

or

The required analysis of capital reserves is due at the RTC next week.

The plaintiff maintains that he never received the detailed grievance filing procedures memo.	The plaintiff maintains that he never received the memo explaining how to file a grievance.

They need to perform an overall product quality improvement plan.

They need to plan ways to improve
the overall quality of their product.

18 Qualify only when necessary.

One sure way to make a sentence longer—and mislead your readers, to
boot—is to be promiscuous with qualifying words and phrases. The
writer wishes, for example, to let employees know that they are in no
danger of being laid off. He could easily write, *You are in no danger of
being laid off*. But this is not what he writes. Deciding to embellish, he
writes, *You are in no immediate danger of being laid off*. The reader (who
reads the words, not the mind) encounters the word *immediate* and must
assume that he is in some other sort of danger. Perhaps he will be laid
off next month or perhaps in the next quarter.

Some qualifiers are so unnecessary that they are ludicrous (*confined
only to* and *including, but not limited to* are prime examples of redundancy).
The reader can hack her way through the ludicrous, but she has no
crystal ball, and when the writer writes, *The explicit conclusions of the
committee are that we should continue the research*, the reader must wonder
about those other conclusions, the implicit ones, at which the writer
hints. But what the writer means, and all he means, is "The committee
concluded that we should continue the research."

Suggest no distinctions where no distinctions exist. Like doublings,
unnecessary qualifiers mislead. They do not mislead the writer, because
the writer knows the truth. They mislead the reader, who does not, and
who is relying on the writer to tell her. All the revisions below do is tell
the unembellished truth.

If we have no plans to change the policy:	~~At this point in time,~~ we have no ~~firm~~ plans to change the policy.
If you own only one mainframe, which happens to be a Zeich:	The ~~Zeich~~ mainframe ~~that we bought last year~~ already needs repair.
If all of the consultants are on-site, and if the only restrictions being discussed are scheduling restrictions:	The ~~on-site~~ consultants favor relaxing the ~~scheduling~~ restrictions.
If you have no evidence to suggest they will ever reveal it, and if they have not "revealed" a phony source:	~~At the present time,~~ they refuse to reveal the ~~actual~~ source of the leak.

If only one regulation is being discussed, and if it will not affect your short-term plans, either:	The ~~aforementioned~~ regulation will not affect our ~~long-term~~ plans.
If you have always believed it, do not intend to indicate that you may someday stop believing it, have had only one hunch, and are discussing only the identity of an industrial spy:	We ~~now~~ believe that our ~~initial~~ hunch ~~regarding the identity of the industrial spy~~ is correct.

⑲ Avoid unnecessary repetition.

"Never repeat words" is another of the false taboos that undermine good writing. Repetition often works. In fact, repeating a word or phrase is a fine idea as long as you repeat for effect. A writer at an electric utility, attempting to convince the developer of a shopping mall to choose electricity (rather than oil or gas) for heating and air conditioning, uses good judgment when she writes,

> Using electricity will result in lower installation costs, lower maintenance costs, and lower fuel costs over the life of the structure.

Because the idea of *lower* is what the writer wishes to emphasize, the reader encounters the word three times. This is effective writing. The alternative sentence below, in which *lower* appears only once, is much less emphatic and persuasive.

> Using electricity will lower not only your installation costs, but also your maintenance costs and fuel costs over the life of the structure.

The trick is to avoid *unnecessary* repetition (i.e., repetition that calls attention to itself or dilutes emphasis because it does not serve to hammer home a point). *HUD issued RFQ G91207 on December 10. HUD's RFQ G91207 sought bids from contractors interested in presenting writing workshops for HUD* is a typical example of unnecessary repetition. All that the writer needed to say was this:

> On December 10, HUD issued RFQ G91207, which sought bids from contractors interested in presenting writing workshops.

Another example of senseless repetition: *The Cost/Benefit Analysis (C/BA) performed in March indicates that additional regulation would serve no useful purpose. There is a strong suggestion from the March C/BA that additional regulation would actually impede productivity by increasing the paperwork burden on small business.* All that the writer needed to say (all that the reader needs) is this:

> The Cost/Benefit Analysis performed in March indicates that additional regulation would serve no purpose. The analysis strongly suggests that the additional paperwork would merely decrease productivity.

Don't forget what the reader already knows. This forgetfulness is what accounts for the unnecessary repetition of words and phrases. Repeat only for effect. If the branch has already been identified as *Special Operations Branch*, the budget has already been characterized as *the proposed FY94 budget*, and the only project mentioned is the *White Winds project*, then repeating those ideas does nothing but clutter the sentence:

> Any cuts to the ~~proposed FY94~~ budget ~~of the Special Operations Branch~~ would force us to eliminate several programs crucial to the ~~White Winds~~ project.

On Being Emphatic

In any sentence, the order of the words largely determines meaning and emphasis. An imprecise order of words opens the door to unintended meanings and magnificent madness. Which of the following (clear) sentences present the reader with a cannibalistic attorney and carrion-consuming biologists?

It was said that his client was eaten alive by the defense attorney.

The defense attorney remarked that his client was "eaten alive."

Because they consume carrion as well as kill their own prey, some biologists regard lions as scavengers.

Because lions eat carrion as well as kill their own prey, some biologists regard them as scavengers.

The order of words will foster clarity or foment ambiguity. Note the ambiguity in the sentences on the left; note how moving a word clarifies the expression.

People whose work requires travel frequently become depressed.

Frequently, people whose work requires travel become depressed.

or

People whose work requires frequent travel become depressed.

Reporting the discovery immediately will create chaos in the scientific community.

Reporting the discovery will immediately create chaos in the scientific community.

or

Immediately reporting the discovery will create chaos in the scientific community.

The order of words will either simplify or complicate reading. In which column below are the sentences easier to understand?

The policy, as it is now written, is, according to the ACLU, unconstitutional and, if enforced, will, when challenged, for the first time, in court, be declared null, void, and illegal.

According to the ACLU, the current policy is unconstitutional and will be declared illegal the first time it is challenged in court.

The economic consequences of forcing small businesses to provide comprehensive medical insurance to all employees are currently unknown.	We do not know the economic consequences of requiring small businesses to provide comprehensive medical insurance to all employees.

The order of the words suggests the intended emphasis. Note how the sentences in the right column better emphasize the annual nature of the adjustment and the urgency of the need.

The cost-of-living index is adjusted on an annual basis by the Commerce Department.	Annually, the Commerce Department adjusts the cost-of-living index.
The errors must be immediately corrected.	The errors must be corrected immediately.

The beginnings and endings of sentences are emphatic. Below, in the examples on the left, both *auditor* and *second quarter of 1993* are deemphasized. The idea of *auditor* is presented as part of an extra phrase, and *second-quarter 1993* is presented as an adjective. If you wish to stress the auditor and the second quarter of 1993, then those ideas must be moved to positions of emphasis. In the revisions on the right, *auditor* becomes the subject, and *the second quarter of 1993* ends the sentence.

The risk, according to the auditor, is minimal.	The auditor believes that the risk is minimal.
We have not received the second-quarter 1993 tax report.	We have not received the tax report for the second quarter of 1993.

You reduce emphasis on an idea when you place it in the middle of a sentence. Below, in the examples on the left, *the last five years* and *relevant* are heavily emphasized. Note how placing these ideas in the middle of the sentences makes them seem less important.

For the last five years, our principal goal has been to improve customer service.	Our principal goal over the last five years has been to improve customer service.
We must stress that the idea is relevant.	We must stress the relevance of the idea.

The order of words takes the place of vocal emphasis. Because the reader doesn't know how you'd stress the words if you were speaking, she relies on their order for a sense of their relative importance. And she reads what you write. If you were speaking, you might stress *yesterday* in such a sentence as *We only received your RFP yesterday*. But the reader doesn't hear that, and if your intent is to express how recently you received the RFP, then you write, *We received the RFP only yesterday*.

Plain style requires that you (1) decide what you're writing about, (2) find the right word for it, (3) use that word as the subject, and (4) tell the truth in simple language. The truth is contained in the verb. Find the precise verb and reveal it as soon as you can.

Remember Technique 8. Don't worry about whether your sentence is active or passive. Do concern yourself with whether you are emphasizing the idea you intend to emphasize. (The reader assumes you've chosen the subject deliberately.) In the example below, if you wish to stress Professor Landris, you will have an active sentence; if you wish to stress what she discovered, you will have a passive one.

Active	*Passive*
Professor Landris discovered a complete skeleton of Allosaurus.	A complete skeleton of Allosaurus was discovered by Professor Landris.

Regardless of whether the resulting sentence is active or passive, pick the precise verb and reveal it. Nothing more frustrates understanding than verbs that are "politely late" to the party. Always organize sentences so that the verb appears as close as possible to the subject.

The techniques that follow will make your writing emphatic.

⟨20⟩ Put words in subject-verb-object order.

The subject-verb-object order of words stresses the right idea, fosters simplicity, and minimizes errors in grammar. If the subject acts, this order of words also improves economy. Below, in the example on the left, the subject (*wolf*) and the verb (*thrives*) are widely separated; the passive construction *endangered by scientists* is not what the writer wishes to convey (nor does he wish to convey that the scientists endangered the wolf several years ago). In the revision, subjects and verbs are side by side; as a result, there are no unintended meanings and the expression is easier to follow. Note that the revision requires two sentences.

The red wolf, thought to be endangered by scientists several years ago in coastal North Carolina, today thrives there.	Several years ago, scientists thought that the red wolf was endangered in coastal North Carolina. Today it thrives there.

Remember, a sentence can be both "correct" and difficult to understand. The goal of a good writer is to write sentences that are correct and clear on the first reading; the subject-verb-object order of words helps make them easy to understand. Below are some common constructions that create needless complexity.

Avoid putting a lot of words between the subject and verb. Instead, place the verb as close as possible to the subject, as in the examples on the right.

Several benefits from the new policy permitting employees to work out of their homes will accrue to us.	Several benefits will result from the new policy permitting employees to work at home.
The ultimate breadth and extent of the toxic spill in the Fairfield area that occurred last week has not yet been determined.	We have not yet determined the ultimate extent of the toxic spill that occurred last week in the Fairfield area.
We will, in the event that premiums for medical insurance continue to skyrocket as they have over the last decade, convert to an HMO.	If medical insurance premiums continue to skyrocket, we will convert to an HMO.
The opportunities for multiple breakthroughs in the field of hydrodynamic research related to energy production increase annually.	In the field of hydrodynamic research related to energy production, opportunities for multiple breakthroughs increase annually.

Refrain from "funhouse" structures, where the writer's "discoveries" jump out at every turn. Minimize punctuation by organizing more deliberately.

The benefits, to my way of thinking, of establishing an office in Italy are manifold.	I believe that we would benefit in many ways from establishing an office in Italy.
This option, unlike the others, will enable us, on a monthly basis, to track our direct costs.	Unlike the other options, this one will enable us to track our direct costs each month.
The CEO, along with the president, is of the opinion that the restructuring, as it is now planned, will increase profitability.	Both the CEO and the president believe that the planned restructuring will increase profits.

Let people do things. Many of the problems in emphasis, clarity, and conciseness will disappear if you let people (and things) act.

Many fears have been raised regarding the possibility of an eruption by Dr. Putkus.

[Is Dr. Putkus a volatile fellow?]
Dr. Putkus has often expressed concerns about the possibility of an eruption.

It is our finding that there was no other option for Mission Control except to abort the launch.

[Note how economy improves.]
We find that Mission Control had no option but to abort the launch.

Racing to meet the deadline, the report was sent by overnight express.

[But the report was not racing.]
Racing to meet the deadline, we sent the report by overnight express.

To be considered for the position, a top-secret clearance must be obtained.

[Clearances aren't considered for positions.]
To be considered for the position, you must obtain a top-secret clearance.

Rather than write lengthy sentences where nothing in particular is emphasized, be willing to give each important idea a sentence of its own. All adults have heard "rules" regarding the maximum length of sentences—twenty words or fewer, fifteen words or fewer—and these should be discarded. They are artificial; some sentences require thirty, forty, or fifty words.

Let emphasis dictate length. Think of an art gallery where one small picture hangs on a large white wall. What would happen to the emphasis on that picture if another were placed beside it? What would happen if two more were added?

["Improved productivity" lost.]
Our new headquarters building, which is scheduled to be completed next year, will enable us to provide each employee with a private office, which should significantly improve productivity.

["Improved productivity" rescued.]
When we move into our new headquarters building next year, each employee will have a private office. As a result, productivity should improve significantly.

[This requires two readings.]
The results of the survey among managers that was conducted to determine the relationship of dollars spent on training to improved productivity last month are summarized below.

[This requires only one reading.]
Last month we surveyed managers to determine the correlation between training dollars and productivity. This report summarizes the results of the survey.

Sentence length is purely a matter of judgment. Just understand the practical consequences of what you do. Length dilutes. Brevity emphasizes.

[One sentence, perfectly "correct," but nothing in particular emphasized.]

Wordiness, jargon, and pretentious language have been creeping into our letters and memos, and this is not good for business, and I want it immediately to stop.

[Three sentences, each idea emphasized.]

Wordiness, jargon, and pretentious language have been creeping into our letters and memos. Such writing hurts business. It must stop immediately.

21 Be judicious with *that* and *which.*

If you had both a hammer and a wrench, and you wanted to tighten a bolt, which tool would you use? Anyone who answers "the hammer" should cease reading and go catch 747s in a butterfly net. Those who believe in using the right tool for the job will distinguish *that* from *which.*

When an idea is essential to meaning, introduce it with *that.* If, for example, you've received five proposals and intend to indicate that a particular one is incomplete, you'd write,

The proposal that arrived this morning is incomplete.

The phrase *that arrived this morning* is essential to the meaning; it specifies which proposal you're talking about. The phrase cannot be cut from the sentence. If it were, the sentence would read, *The proposal is incomplete—* and that is ambiguous, since you've received five proposals.

When an idea is extra, introduce it with *which. Which* is used to combine two sentences when the writer intends to deemphasize one. If you've received only one proposal, the proposal happens to be incomplete, and it arrived this morning, you could write two short sentences: *The proposal arrived this morning. It is incomplete.* Or you could use a *which* clause to combine the two ideas:

deemphasized

The proposal, which arrived this morning, is incomplete.

deemphasized

The proposal, which is incomplete, arrived this morning.

In the former, the main point of the sentence is *The proposal is incomplete.* Because you've received only one proposal, you do not need to specify which proposal you're talking about; thus, the phrase *which arrived this morning* is an extra (or "parenthetical") idea. It could be cut from the sentence and so it is punctuated. In the latter, the main point is *The proposal arrived this morning.* The phrase *which is incomplete* is the extra thought now; it could be cut from the sentence and so it is punctuated.

Don't use *which* if you mean *that*. Without punctuation, *which* clauses can be understood as *that* clauses. Dire problems in clarity occur when *which* is used as a substitute for *that*.

Ambiguous:	The task force is searching for the F-117 which was lost over the Red Sea. [*How many F-117s have been lost? One? More than one?*]
Clear:	The task force is searching for the F-117 that was lost over the Red Sea. [*As opposed to the one lost over the Indian Ocean or somewhere else.*]
Clear:	The task force is searching for the F-117, which was lost over the Red Sea. [*Only one F-117 has been lost. By the way, it was lost over the Red Sea.*]

Because the world teems with committees, you need to specify precisely which committee you're talking about, and you would write

essential phrase
The committee that has jurisdiction on the issue is the Senate Ethics Committee.

The phrase *that has jurisdiction on the issue* is necessary to the meaning of the sentence. The phrase cannot be cut; if it were cut, you'd have *The committee is the Senate Ethics Committee* (which is a tautological and senseless statement).

On the other hand, because there is only one Senate Ethics Committee, you would write,

deemphasized
The Senate Ethics Committee, which convened last night, voted to censure the senator from Pennsylvania for his unnecessarily harsh treatment of the witness.

The phrase *which convened last night* isn't necessary to complete the meaning of the sentence. It could easily be cut; if it were, you'd have *The Senate Ethics Committee voted to censure the senator from Pennsylvania for his*

In fact, the attorney is not unlikely to file another appeal. We expect her to do so by the end of the week.

Despite Dr. Vork's claim, it is not unusual for the species to be seen so far north. Studies over the past twenty years confirm dozens of sightings as far north as Panama.

The effects of the regulation were not unforeseen. Several administrators vigorously opposed it, insisting that it would stifle competition.

Besides contributing to wordiness and ambiguity, *not* can spoil the tone of communication. Writers inadvertently lose readers—and businesses lose customers—with such sentences as *We will not process your claim at this time because you did not include the three estimates.* A civilized writer, who by definition empathizes with the reader, would recast that sentence so that it tells the reader something positive: *After we receive the three estimates, we will promptly process your claim.*

Use *not* whenever you must. Just make sure that no other word or phrasing will do. If an experiment *does not prove* something, it hardly *disproves* the thing (though it could *fail to prove*); if you are *not in favor* of a proposal, it is silly to *disfavor* it (though if you mean you *object* to it, you should write that).

In the sentences below, *not* and *not un-* constructions impair clarity. Note how the assertions in the examples on the right improve tone, clarify meaning, and foster simplicity.

We did not choose to continue the project.	We chose to end the project.
It is not infrequent that the project manager does not accurately estimate costs.	The project manager frequently underestimates costs.
They did not remember that they were not supposed to lock the emergency door.	They forgot to leave the emergency door unlocked.
The jury did not take all of the evidence into consideration and was not able to reach a verdict.	The jury overlooked some of the evidence and was unable to reach a verdict.
He does not believe in the existence of quarks.	He doubts that quarks exist.
	or
	He refutes the existence of quarks.
	or
	He denies the existence of quarks.

unnecessarily harsh treatment of the witness. Note that the *which* clause requires punctuation.

Ambiguous:	The EPA contract which we won last month will double our revenue.
Clear:	The EPA contract that we won last month will double our revenue. [*You have more than one EPA contract, and this specifies the one you're talking about.*]
Clear:	The EPA contract, which we won last month, will double our revenue. [*There is only one EPA contract; by the way, we won it last month.*]
Ambiguous:	Firearms which are banned in the District of Columbia can easily be bought in Virginia.
Clear:	Firearms that are banned in the District of Columbia can easily be bought in Virginia. [*Certain firearms are banned in D.C.*]
Clear:	Firearms, which are banned in the District of Columbia, can easily be bought in Virginia. [*All firearms are banned in D.C.*]
Ambiguous:	Robots which replace people would be outlawed by this bill.
Clear:	Robots, which replace people, would be outlawed by this bill. [*The bill would outlaw all robots; all robots replace people.*]
Clear:	Robots that replace people would be outlawed by this bill. [*The bill would outlaw only certain robots—the ones that replace people.*]

22 Use discretion when omitting *that* and *which*.

That and *which* are often unnecessary; when they are, they may be cut with impunity. But when are they unnecessary?

Any word is unnecessary when it is so fiercely implied that a practical reading would infer it. *That,* used to specify, is an understood word in sentences like the ones below.

The species she discovered in Costa Rica will be named *Aurora elii.*

The argument we found most persuasive was the one about how people truly read.

The strategy we adopted last year is beginning to pay off.

The polygraph test she took last month was "inconclusive."

Emphasis and economy often improve when you convert *that* clauses to adjectives.

The procedure that is currently in place is unproductive.	The current procedure is unproductive.
The inspection that we performed last week revealed no structural damage.	Last week's inspection revealed no structural damage.
They received a contract extension that will last for six months.	They received a six-month extension to the contract.
The legislation will cripple the economies of states that produce coal.	The legislation will cripple the economies of coal-producing states.

Include *that* to prevent misreading. Include the word to introduce an indirect quotation, or when the sense is "about," as in the following sentences.

[*A paraphrase of his exact words.*] He remarked he saw little to choose between the candidates.	[*The paraphrasing instantly revealed.*] He remarked that he saw little to choose between the candidates.
[*A paraphrase of their exact words.*] They responded we have a serious conflict of interest and we should reveal the affiliation.	[*If they said both things.*] They responded that we have a serious conflict of interest and that we should reveal the affiliation.
[*"We assume their liabilities" is misleading.*] We assume their liabilities exceed their assets.	[*We assume something "about" them.*] We assume that their liabilities exceed their assets.
[*"Note the technique" is misleading.*] Note the technique requires good judgment from the writer.	[*Note something "about" the technique.*] Note that the technique requires good judgment from the writer.

When you use a *so* and provide a result, include *that* for clarity, as on the right.

The device fails so often it is not only useless, but dangerous.	The device fails so often that it is not only useless, but dangerous.
We were so sure of winning the contract we hired seven additional analysts.	We were so sure of winning the contract that we hired seven additional analysts.
The sentence was so ambiguous it had three different meanings.	The sentence was so ambiguous that it had three different meanings.

The project was so well managed it was brought in well under budget.	The contract was managed so well that it was brought in under budget.
Any word is unnecessary when it is so fiercely implied a practical reading would infer it.	Any word is unnecessary when it is so fiercely implied that a practical reading would infer it.

In the middle of a sentence, *which* may often be cut with impunity. Punctuation will indicate that an idea is parenthetical (as *which* clauses always are).

The company, which was founded in 1950, finally went public in 1990.	The company, founded in 1950, finally went public in 1990.
The agreement, which was signed last week, will protect us from sudden cancellations.	The agreement (signed last week) will protect us from sudden cancellations.
The shipment, which we received yesterday, contained no quarter-inch plywood.	The shipment, received yesterday, contained no quarter-inch plywood.
This report, which is comprehensible only after three readings, must have been written in great haste.	This report—comprehensible only after three readings—must have been written in great haste.
Her opinion, which is shared by everyone on the committee, is that we must increase advertising.	Her opinion, shared by everyone on the committee, is that we must increase advertising.

If you believe that emphasis would be improved, convert *which* clauses to adjectives. Note how this technique enables the writer to place the verb beside the subject.

The organization, which is based in Geneva, is a clearinghouse for weapons technology.	The Geneva-based organization is a clearinghouse for weapons technology.
Their performance, which has been exemplary, has doubled our sales.	Their exemplary performance has doubled our sales.
The terrain, which is rugged, is used by NASA scientists to simulate lunar conditions.	The rugged terrain is used by NASA scientists to simulate lunar conditions.
The company's philosophy, which is that you shoot first and aim later, has given it a reputation for inconsistency.	The company's shoot-first-and-aim-later philosophy has given it a reputation for inconsistency.

23 **Place modifiers precisely.**

In English, the meaning of an expression depends largely on the order of the words. There is a vast difference, after all, between the following sentences.

We saw a film about preventing explosions in the conference room.	In the conference room, we saw a film about preventing explosions.
After being convicted of embezzlement, the defense attorney said he and his client would probably appeal.	After his client was convicted of embezzlement, the defense attorney said they would probably appeal.
On her own time, she has been acting as a mentally ill advocate.	On her own time, she has been acting as an advocate for the mentally ill.
I saw the rare lemur staring at the moon with my own eyes.	With my own eyes, I saw the rare lemur staring at the moon.

Meaning isn't the only thing at stake. A well-organized sentence will be read and understood effortlessly; a haphazard order of words obstructs sense and requires too much effort from the reader. Sentences like the ones below require several readings because modifying phrases have been spewed out and left to rot where they landed.

> He discovered the technique in Switzerland that we use to separate molecules by accident forty years ago.

> She claimed that she was singled out for abuse from January through April by her manager without reason.

> We must insist that you pay the invoice for the shipment that we mailed on October 19 by December 1.

Make sure that each modifying expression relates unequivocally to the word you intend it to describe. Organize the words so that each modifier appears right beside the word it describes. When modifiers are loosely placed, ambiguity results:

> The consultant has been trying to get us to extend his contract for two months.

Because the phrase *for two months* has been carelessly placed, the sentence has three (equally plausible) interpretations:

For two months, the consultant has been asking us to extend his contract.

The consultant is requesting a two-month extension to his contract.

The consultant is asking us to extend his two-month contract.

The next few pages will alert you to the common ways in which modifiers cause confusion, ambiguity, and difficulty. The solution to each problem is the same—place the modifier beside the word you intend it to describe.

▪ Modifiers that begin sentences bear careful watching. Everyone has encountered the bizarre images that result when modifiers "dangle." (The one in the sentence below describes a very enthusiastic repairman.)

Spitting sparks and whipping wildly from side to side, the repairman attempted to reconnect the downed power line.

When you begin a sentence with a modifying phrase, make certain that the next idea is what you intend that phrase to modify.

Hurrying through the report, an important detail was overlooked by the auditor.

[*The auditor, not the detail, hurried through the report.*]
Hurrying through the report, the auditor overlooked an important detail.

Because they can lift fifty times their weight, biologists regard the ants as the strongest of all animals.

[*Few biologists are so impressive.*]
Because ants can lift fifty times their weight, biologists regard them as the strongest of all animals.

Flying at 40,000 feet, the missile silos were impossible to detect.

[*Missile silos never behave in this manner.*]
From 40,000 feet, we could not detect the missile silos.

After being planted in the Rose Garden, the First Lady called the bush "a small piece of England."

[*The First Lady wasn't planted in the Rose Garden. The bush was.*]
After the bush was planted in the Rose Garden, the First Lady called it "a small piece of England."

While lethal in large doses, the study suggests that the drug may be beneficial in small doses.

[*Truly, some studies are lethal in large doses, but the lethality here should apply to the drug.*]
The study suggests that the drug— while lethal in large doses—may be beneficial in small doses.

Unlike most manned space vehicles, the chief engineer claims that the AVR-20 can remain in orbitation mode for one full year.

[*The chief engineer may or may not be gratified by such a comparison.*]
The chief engineer claims that the AVR-20 (unlike most manned space vehicles) can remain in orbit for one full year.

Screaming their slogans at one another, the police dispersed the opposing protesters.

[*The protesters were the ones screaming.*]
Screaming their slogans at one another, the opposing protesters were dispersed by the police.

Reeling from a series of setbacks, the regulators called the company "a financial basket case."

[*But the regulators were not reeling.*]
The company is reeling from a series of setbacks; regulators have called it "a financial basket case."

▪ Modifiers that end sentences bear careful watching. More often than not, phrases that end sentences are merely "tacked on" and can be understood to relate to two (or more) ideas. Observe the unintended meanings and ambiguities in the sentences in the left column; note that each revision either entirely rewrites the expression or places the modifier right beside the appropriate word.

Serious allegations have been raised regarding sexual harrassment by Professor Hill.

[*Professor Hill raised the allegations.*]
Professor Hill has raised serious allegations regarding sexual harassment.

We demanded their commitment to pull their troops out of Kuwait by noon on Saturday.

[*We did not intend to demand that the Iraqis remove their troops by a certain time, but that they commit by a certain time.*]
We demanded that they commit, by noon on Saturday, to pull their troops out of Kuwait.

He wrote that the satellite must have fallen into the ocean in his report.

[*The report contained no ocean.*]
In his report, he wrote that the satellite must have fallen into the ocean.

When we checked the files, we found records of employees that were out of date.

[*The employees aren't out of date.*]
When we checked the files, we found out-of-date records of employees.

We saw the Bigfoot looking at us through high-powered binoculars.

[*And no doubt the Bigfoot was chuckling.*]
Through high-powered binoculars, we saw the Bigfoot looking at us.

You can see our new headquarters building driving up Interstate 270.

[*Should you be careful not to blink?*]
From I-270, you can see our new headquarters building.

Many items are stored in the warehouse of great historical significance.

[*The warehouse itself isn't that important.*]
Many items of great historical significance are stored in the warehouse.

Old floppy disks will be collected by secretaries of every size.

[*Why is the size of the secretaries relevant?*]
Secretaries will collect old floppy disks of every size.

We watched the space shuttle lift off from the observation bunker.

[*It must have been a warming experience.*]
From the observation bunker, we watched the space shuttle lift off.

They warned us that competition would be stiff at the outset.

[*But true competition remains stiff.*]
At the outset, they warned us that competition would be stiff.

▪ Often, a modifier in the middle of a sentence is ambiguous because it can relate to the idea that precedes it or to the one that follows it. The alert (i.e., sensible and deliberate) writer places each prepositional phrase where it belongs. Observe how the capricious placement of phrases in the examples in the left column can make simple thoughts sound like something overheard in the Twilight Zone.

He was stung by the parking lot on the left side of his neck.

Near the parking lot, he was stung on the left side of his neck.

There was never any reason in his mind to hesitate.

In his mind, there was never any reason to hesitate.

She never thought she'd be promoted to vice president in her wildest dreams.

In her wildest dreams, she never thought she'd be promoted to vice president.

The top-secret files are on the desk in his briefcase.

The top-secret files are in his briefcase on the desk.

This stock in her opinion will double in two years.

In her opinion, this stock will double in two years.

The FTC believes this advertising in several ways to be unfair.

The FTC believes this advertising is unfair in several ways.

Our goal for ten years has been to simplify writing.

For ten years, our goal has been to simplify writing.
or
Our ten-year goal has been to simplify writing.

Simplifying the procedure soon will save us thousands of dollars.

By simplifying the procedure soon, we will save thousands of dollars.
or
Simplifying the procedure will soon save us thousands of dollars.

Their remarkable record in such ventures of success is due to hard work.

Their remarkable record of success in such ventures is due to hard work.
or
Hard work accounts for their remarkable record of success in such ventures.

She states that lewd comments were made by the water cooler on the way down the hall.

She states that she heard lewd comments as she passed the water cooler.

Their plan to increase hydroelectric output in any event will prove costly.

In any event, their plan to increase hydroelectric output will prove costly.

Our revenue forecast for six months has been undergoing revision.

For six months, we have been revising our revenue forecast.
or
We have been revising our six-month revenue forecast.

• *Which* clauses bear careful watching. Place each *which* clause right beside the word it actually describes. Loose placements can result in wild ideas like those in the left column.

The new policy will begin next year, which has been approved by the board of directors.

[*"Next year" does not require approval from the board.*]
The new policy, which will begin next year, has been approved by the board of directors.

We learned a technique in the training we attended last week, which will prove useful.

[*"Technique," not "week," will prove useful.*]
We learned a useful technique in last week's training.

The Senate blames the stalemate on the House, which shows no signs of being resolved.	[*"No signs of being resolved" applies to "stalemate."*] The Senate blames the House for the stalemate, which shows no signs of being resolved.
Biologists report seeing snow leopards in the Himalayas, which they believed were extinct years ago.	[*The Himalayas are in no danger of extinction.*] Biologists report seeing snow leopards (which were believed to be extinct years ago) in the Himalayas.

▪ *That* clauses also bear careful watching. Like other modifying phrases, a *that* clause must be placed right beside the word it describes.

The investment was ill-advised that they made in robotics.	The investment that they made in robotics was ill-advised. *Better:* Their investment in robotics was ill-advised.
Several remarks were made by the engineer that we found surprising.	The engineer made several remarks that we found surprising. *Better:* The engineer made several surprising remarks.
They plan to take several measures in the coming year that will immunize them against fluctuations in interest rates.	Next year they plan to take several measures that will protect them from fluctuations in interest rates.
Numerous errors were made by the company in its proposal that claims it believes in "excellence."	The company that claims it believes in "excellence" made numerous errors in its proposal.

▪ *Only, even,* and *just* bear careful watching. These three words, like hoboes, tend to wander around and camp wherever they choose. For the sake of precision, place them right before the idea you intend them to modify.

The expression:	*logically means:*
I only watch football on Sundays.	I don't do anything else on Sundays.
I watch football only on Sundays.	I don't watch football on any other day.
I watch only football on Sundays.	I don't watch anything else on Sundays.
We only requested the arbitration yesterday.	We merely requested (not demanded) it.

We requested the arbitration only yesterday.

Smoking is only allowed in designated areas.

Smoking is allowed only in designated areas.

We only decided to renovate the executive lounge.

We decided to renovate only the executive lounge.

The prosecution's only evidence is circumstantial.

The prosecution's evidence is only circumstantial.

The CEO was not even aware of the lawsuit.

The CEO was unaware even of the lawsuit.

Even the CEO was unaware of the lawsuit.

It's frightening even to contemplate a slight decrease in revenue.

It's frightening to contemplate even a slight decrease in revenue.

The species was even observed mating underwater.

The species was observed mating even underwater.

The bank protested even the positive findings of the audit.

The bank even protested the positive findings of the audit.

We've just received the proposal.

We've received just the proposal.

Dr. Coombs wrote just the report.

Dr. Coombs just wrote the report.

It's been only one day since our request.

It's not "encouraged" or "advised."

It's allowed nowhere else.

We merely decided to do it, as opposed to signing a contract.

We decided to renovate the lounge and to renovate nothing else.

The prosecution has but one bit of evidence, which happens to be circumstantial.

All of the prosecution's evidence is circumstantial.

He didn't know about it.

He was unaware of a lot of other things.

This is surprising (since he, of all people, should be aware of it).

The mere act of contemplating this prospect is frightening.

Any decrease in revenue, no matter how slight, is a frightening prospect.

Someone actually saw this; in other words, it isn't myth or hearsay.

The insatiable species mates underwater, as well as on land.

Besides protesting the negative findings, the bank protested the positive ones.

The bank did not merely complain, but went so far as to protest the findings.

We recently received it.

We've received only the proposal, not the necessary supporting documents.

That's all she wrote.

She merely wrote (not edited) the report.

or

She recently completed the report.

■ *Either . . . or* and *neither . . . nor* expressions also bear careful watching. When these words are out of balance, the reader has to read the sentence twice. The problem is typified by the following sentence:

> Either the FDIC must raise funds or reduce the extent of insurance coverage.

When the reader encounters *Either the FDIC,* he expects the *or* phrase to suggest another organization—*Either the FDIC or the RTC* must do thus-and-such. Instead, the sentence compares the FDIC to the act of reducing. In this sentence, the writer intends to balance *raise* and *reduce*:

> The FDIC must either raise funds or reduce the extent of insurance coverage.

The technique is simple and consistent: Place *either* (or *neither*) immediately before the word you intend to compare; place *or* (or *nor*) immediately before the word compared. The examples in the left column are imprecise; the revised sentences are precise.

Either they overlooked the deadline or ignored it.	They either overlooked the deadline or ignored it.
Expenses must either be reduced or revenue must be increased.	We must either reduce expenses or increase revenue.
The company can neither explain the cost overrun nor the delay.	The company can explain neither the cost overrun nor the delay.
The report neither contains all the relevant data nor the most current data.	This report contains neither all the relevant data nor the most current data.
Either we change our policy or risk being censured for violating EEO regulations.	Either we change our policy or we risk being censured for violating EEO regulations.
	or
	We either change our policy or risk being censured for violating EEO regulations.
The species is either extinct or it exists now only in inaccessible locales.	The species is either extinct or exists now only in inaccessible locales.
They neither accepted the apology nor the offer of settlement.	They accepted neither the apology nor the offer of settlement.
Either the Senate will take up the issue or it will be taken up in the House.	Either the Senate or the House will take up the issue.

24 **Hyphenate to create the appropriate emphasis.**

Because readers pay particular attention to the way a sentence starts and concludes, any word in these positions receives a natural emphasis, or "weight." It's as though a bright spotlight shines on the idea that ends a sentence—and the practical writer will not end a sentence arbitrarily. She will be deliberate and end with the word that deserves emphasis. Consider the sentence below.

> The executives have gone on a retreat that will last for four days.

That's an emphatic sentence if the writer wishes to emphasize *executives* and *four days*. But it isn't an emphatic sentence if she wishes to emphasize *executives* and *retreat*. *Retreat* is buried and thus receives very little stress. If the writer wishes to highlight *retreat*, then she needs to place that word in the spotlight at the end of the sentence—and knowing how to hyphenate enables her to.

> The executives have gone on a four-day retreat.

As you read the examples below, notice how a word's importance is magnified when that word appears at the end of the sentence. Notice also that we hyphenate when the phrase precedes the noun. All of the sentences are "correct." The question is: How precisely does the order of words capture and present the writer's intended emphasis? Only the writer can answer that—but she should know the technique that will give her both options.

[Emphasizes "long term."]
They plan to establish a partnership that will extend over the long term.

[Emphasizes "high income."]
The new taxes are aimed at professionals who earn a high income.

[Emphasizes "end of the year."]
Enclosed is a copy of our analysis for the end of the year.

[Emphasizes "none too robust."]
The latest statistics indicate a recovery that is none too robust.

[Emphasizes "your own pocket."]
The new plan will reduce the expenses you pay out of your own pocket.

[Emphasizes "partnership."]
They plan to establish a long-term partnership.

[Emphasizes "professionals."]
The new taxes are aimed at high-income professionals.

[Emphasizes "analysis."]
Enclosed is a copy of our end-of-year analysis.

[Emphasizes "recovery."]
The latest statistics indicate a none-too-robust recovery.

[Emphasizes "expenses."]
The new plan will reduce your out-of-pocket expenses.

Hyphenating also enables the writer to avoid suggesting something she doesn't intend. In *We were delighted by the forecast for six months*, the delight probably didn't last for half a year: We were delighted by *the six-month forecast*. In *His manager has been urging him to take a vacation for three weeks*, either the manager has been urging for three weeks or the manager has been urging him to take a *three-week vacation*.

As useful as it is, the hyphen is notoriously misunderstood and prone to abuse. When the special of the day is half of a baked chicken, but the menu says *half-baked chicken*, the restauranteur will marvel at the brisk sale of beef; when the owner of a burned-out store is captioned, on the television news, as a *burned-out storeowner*, viewers will wonder what his need for a vacation has to do with the arson they've been hearing about.

What the Hyphen Does

The hyphen connects things. It can (1) connect prefixes to words (*re-sign, anti-inflammatory, pro-choice*) to form a different word and (2) connect words to form a single noun (the *president-elect*, a state of *self-consciousness*). Guidance on these usages is available in dictionaries and style guides. We are concerned here with the third major use of the hyphen—the one that requires the writer's judgment as she invents compound adjectives ("unit modifiers") on the spot.

Consider, for example, the position of the writer who has written, *Executives have responded favorably to the new format, which is easy to scan.* She had ended her sentence with—and has therefore emphasized—an afterthought (the parenthetical *which is easy to scan*). Her sentence is perfectly correct. But let's suppose she wishes to emphasize *format*. She knows that it's the writer's job to direct the reader's understanding, and thus she needs to change the order of the words. So she writes, *Executives have responded favorably to the new, easy-to-scan format.*

You won't find *easy-to-scan* in any dictionary or style guide. For flexibility—the flexibility that enables a writer to emphasize the right idea—an understanding of technique is crucial.

How to Use the Hyphen

Consider the following sentence:

We need to reassess our goals for the third quarter.

The words are in normal parts-of-speech order: *third* is an adjective and *quarter* is a noun (as they ordinarily are) and thus no hyphen is required.

If the writer wishes to emphasize *the third quarter*, then this is a fine expression. But if the writer wishes to emphasize *goals*, then she will have to alter the order of words and write, *We need to reassess our third-quarter goals*.

When we write the words in that order, we have changed the way *third* and *quarter* are behaving: *quarter* is no longer a noun. It has been wrenched out of its traditional role and has become part of an adjective modifying *goals*. The hyphen is used to indicate that in this sentence *third-quarter* is a unit.

It's the same principle over and over. When you have a phrase like *a suspension of five days*, you can convert it to *a five-day suspension*. When wondering whether to hyphenate, just ask yourself, "Is it a five suspension *and* a day suspension?" Clearly, it isn't. *Five-day* is a unit of thought. Those two words are behaving like a single adjective, and they come before the noun. And so you hyphenate.

In another example, we have *boosters that use solid fuel*. In that phrase, *fuel* is a noun and *solid* is an adjective. If we convert the phrase to *solid-fuel boosters*, we've altered the way *fuel* behaves in the sentence; it's now part of an adjective. We hyphenate because they are not "solid" boosters *and* "fuel" boosters.

Here we have *adjustments to reflect the cost of living*, and the phrase can become *cost-of-living adjustments*. We hyphenate *cost-of-living* because the three words are behaving like an adjective. We aren't talking about "cost" adjustments, "of" adjustments, *and* "living" adjustments.

And here we have *records that are out of date*. That's fine, but if we wish to emphasize *records*, we write *out-of-date records*. They aren't "out" records, "of" records, *and* "date" records. And so we hyphenate the phrase.

That's basically all there is to it. Our *capability for verifying intelligence* becomes our *intelligence-verifying capability*. An Olympic sprint of one hundred meters becomes a *100-meter dash*, a cup that holds four ounces becomes a *4-ounce cup*, and a beam that is six feet long becomes a *6-foot beam* (it isn't a "six" beam *and* a "foot" beam). Diskettes with a high density are *high-density diskettes*, objectives for the near term are *near-term objectives*, and an organization that is strapped for cash is a *cash-strapped organization*. Bonds that are rated AAA become *AAA-rated bonds*; a dog that can detect explosives by sniffing becomes an *explosive-sniffing dog*— not, we hope, an explosive sniffing one.

Follow Accepted Usage

The hyphen connects words to indicate that they form a unit, and writers need to hyphenate only when the reader wouldn't instantly recognize the words to be a unit. There's no need to hyphenate *law enforcement* officer and *federal budget* deficit because those phrases are so commonly seen that they are understood to form units. Readers recognize *life insurance* company, *long distance* bill, and *atomic energy* program; hyphens do not aid clarity in familiar phrases and may safely be omitted.

25 Keep equal ideas "parallel."

When ideas are of equal importance, a sentence should express them in identical structures. Consider, for example, the following (difficult) sentence:

> We arrived on the site, interviewed the supervisor, and it is thought that the work will be completed on schedule.

Besides being awkward, that sentence is ambiguous. Who's doing the thinking—the writer or the supervisor? Since the sentence begins with two verb constructions (arrived, interviewed), we make the last idea fit the pattern by finding a third verb:

>   *1*   *2*   *3*
> We arrived on the site, interviewed the supervisor, and determined that the work will be completed on schedule.

If the ideas below were on an old-fashioned scale, would they balance?

> It is far more prudent to invest the dividend than distributing it.

The ideas of investing and distributing are expressed in different ways in that sentence. Since they are being directly compared, they should appear in identical structures:

> It is far more prudent to invest the dividend than to distribute it.
> *or*
> Investing the dividend is far more prudent than distributing it.

▪ When you compare two or more ideas, make sure that the ideas are comparably presented, as they are in the examples on the right.

We have neither received the final report nor the interim findings.	We have received neither the final report nor the interim findings.

They are not opening an office in London but in Edinburgh.

They are opening an office not in London but in Edinburgh.

Not only was the training practical, but it was relevant.

The training was not only practical but relevant.

They are not only concerned about imports but about fluctuations in the value of the dollar.

They are concerned not only about imports but about fluctuations in the value of the dollar.

The companies have both agreed to the merger and reorganization.

The companies have agreed both to the merger and to the reorganization.

or

The companies have agreed to both the merger and the reorganization.

We have both decided to reduce indirect costs and direct costs.

We have decided to reduce both direct and indirect costs.

■ When you list ideas of equal importance, keep the ideas parallel, as they are in the right column.

[*These three nouns should not be parallel.*]
The Hotline provides support to those suffering from addiction, their families, and friends.

[*"Support to" is made parallel.*]
The Hotline provides support not only to those suffering from addiction, but also to their families and friends.

[*Two nouns and a conditional phrase.*]
We are concerned about relevance, validity, and whether the testimony is credible.

[*Three nouns, if all apply to "evidence."*]
We are concerned about the relevance, validity, and credibility of the evidence.

[*One infinitive, one "-ing" verb, and a noun.*]
Careful analysis of the photographs is necessary to detect troops, for verifying the placement of reserves, and the identification of movement.

[*Three infinitives.*]
Analyze the photographs carefully to detect troops, to verify the placement of reserves, and to identify movement.

[*Capricious shifting from passive to active forces reader to wonder whether "we" are responsible for all three activities.*]

[*Three verbs, if "we" must do all three.*]

The issue must be defined, we must research it, and a report on the matter must be produced as soon as possible.

As soon as possible, we must define, research, and report on the issue.

[*Two prepositional phrases and a noun phrase.*]

[*Three nouns.*]

You are to be commended for your diligence, for your compassion, and the professional manner in which you handled the difficult situation.

You are to be commended for your diligence, compassion, and professionalism in this difficult situation.

[*One infinitive and a noun phrase.*]

[*Two infinitives.*]

To foster a professional image and for the improvement of customer service, we are installing an 800 number.

To foster a professional image and to improve customer service, we are installing an 800 number.

[*One simple verb and one "-ing" verb.*]

[*Two simple verbs.*]

Problems in clarity will be minimized if you write with verbs and by paying attention to the order of words.

You will minimize problems in clarity if you write with verbs and pay attention to the order of words.

[*One infinitive and one "-ing" verb.*]

[*Two infinitives.*]

The purposes of the trip were to see the effects of the bombardment firsthand and assessing the extent of the damage.

The purposes of the trip were to see the effects of the bombardment firsthand and to assess the extent of the damage.

[*One "-ing" verb and one infinitive.*]

[*Two "-ing" verbs.*]

The project superintendent's responsibilities include writing a weekly report and to ensure that the work is on schedule.

The project superintendent's responsibilities include writing a weekly report and ensuring that the work is on schedule.

[*One preposition and one noun.*]

[*Two precise verbs.*]

Inside each of us is something worth expression and necessary to be expressed.

Inside each of us is something that both deserves and demands expression.

■ Some ideas do not belong in parallel structures. The capricious "cramming in" of ideas can suggest a meaning other than the one you intend. In the sentence below, did the regulators say one thing, or both?

The regulators stated that the company took unfair advantage of its market position, and we have a good chance to win if we sue.

Some readers will assume (naturally enough) that the regulators said both things; others will assume that the regulators said only the first thing and that the writer then expresses his own opinion.

If the regulators said both things, then the ideas should be made parallel:

> The regulators stated that the company took unfair advantage of its market position and that we have a good chance to win if we sue.

If the regulators said only the first thing, then the meaning requires two sentences:

> The regulators stated that the company took unfair advantage of its market position. We have a good chance to win if we sue.

Here are some additional examples.

[*Did the biologist say one thing, or both?*]
The biologist said that the animal was believed to be extinct, but it has been seen recently in the Kenyala Forest.

[*If the biologist said both things.*]
The biologist said that the animal was believed to be extinct but that it has been seen recently in the Kenyala Forest.

[*If the biologist said only the first thing, then the meaning requires two sentences.*]
The biologist said that the animal was believed to be extinct. It has, however, been seen recently in the Kenyala Forest.

[*Does the contract stipulate both things?*]
The contract stipulates that we must supply the materials, and we must ship them within thirty days.

[*If the contract stipulates both.*]
The contract stipulates that we must supply and ship the materials within thirty days.

[*If the contract stipulates only the first thing, then the expression requires two sentences.*]
The contract stipulates that we must supply the materials. If we are to meet our timetable, we must ship the materials within thirty days.

■ Remember also that in a sea of ideas, emphasis always drowns. When you decide that an idea deserves emphasis, put it in a separate sentence.

[*What the reader reads is crammed into one unemphatic sentence.*]
After interviewing the applicants, we decided to increase the salary level of the position and to offer it to Dr. Struthers.

[*What the writer means requires two sentences.*]
After interviewing the applicants, we decided to increase the salary level of the position. Only by doing so can we attract Dr. Struthers, the most qualified candidate.

[*"Before you leave" cannot live in the same atmosphere as "when you arrive."*]
When you arrive at the facility, make sure to show your identification, sign in, go immediately to the briefing room, and secure all classified materials before you leave.

[*These ideas require separate sentences for both clarity and emphasis.*]
When you arrive, show your identification, sign in, and go immediately to the briefing room. Be sure to secure all classified materials before you leave.

26 Don't vary terms without reason.

"Vary your terms" is another of those instructions that makes good sense in eighth grade (when we are trying to increase vocabulary) and makes little sense in business writing. The following example is preposterous:

> The recent rainy weather in Honduras will increase the price of bananas. Consumers will soon begin paying nearly twice as much for *the curvy yellow fruit.*

"Elegant variation," which is variation for the sake of variety (or for the writer's own amusement), sometimes makes the reader laugh but most often leaves him scratching his head. Consider this confusing example:

> The policy, as amended, provides for employees to purchase stock at a discount. The new procedure enables you to buy the shares at their beginning-of-year value anytime in the year. The protocol ensures that the equities, when negotiated, can be acquired at a price lower than the market value of the shares at the time of the purchase.

The question isn't whether the reader can understand this. The question is: How much effort should the reader need to make? In that paragraph, and in countless paragraphs like it, understanding is obstructed by the irresponsible varying of terms. *Policy* becomes *procedure* and then *protocol*. *Stock* begins as *stock* but shifts to *shares*, then *equities*, and then back to *shares*. The idea of "buying" is introduced sensibly enough as *purchase*, shifts to *buy*, then staggers into *negotiated*, and lurches into *acquired*. Here's a sensible revision:

> By permitting you to buy our stock anytime in the year at its beginning-of-year price, the policy offers you a chance to make a nice profit. If, for example, the shares were worth $30 on January 1 and are worth $45 in October, you could buy 100 shares at $30 apiece, sell them, and make an instant $1,500 profit.

Call things by their right names. If it is a pencil in paragraph one, it should remain a pencil in paragraph two, not a *writing instrument*, a *Venus Number Two*, a *handheld wooden scribing device*, or (courtesy of the U.S. Army, the folks who have brought us *wood interdental stimulator* for *toothpick* and *combat emplacement evacuator* for *shovel*) a *manually mobile encrypting tool*. No colonel, in haste to finish his paperwork and unable to find a pencil, has ever cried, "Lieutenant! Get me a manually mobile encrypting tool *now!*" Those ten syllables simply take too long when all he wants is a two-syllable pencil. The colonel demands a *pencil*. If the lieutenant responds (as lieutenants sometimes do), "Sir, do you mean a manually mobile encrypting tool?" then the colonel is right to bust him, court-martial him, and reassign him to the mopping-up detail in the Skunk Pill lab.

27 **Vary terms only to avoid undue repetition.**

Repetition is a fault in writing only when a word or phrase calls inappropriate attention to itself. Does the idea deserve repetition? If it does, repeat it to emphasize it. If it doesn't, then you should find a way to avoid repeating it. Simply beware of stretching so far that you (1) lose the reader, (2) make the reader laugh, (3) make the reader snort with impatience, or (4) contrive a phrase that would never be uttered in ordinary speech.

When you vary nouns, steer by the star of simplicity. Whenever a pronoun would do, use a pronoun. For example, rather than write,

> The lounge on the sixth floor will be closed during the week of September 21. The lounge will reopen on September 28.

it is much simpler to write,

> The lounge on the sixth floor will be closed during the week of September 21. It will reopen on September 28.

Here there is no need to substitute a phrase like *the room, the area,* or *the popular spot* for *the lounge.* In the revised sentence, *it* refers clearly to the lounge; *it* is the simplest choice. In the example below, *they* is the simple choice. Rather than write,

> As written, the procedures are very difficult to understand. These procedures should be clarified and simplified.

it is much simpler to write,

> As written, the procedures are very difficult to understand. They should be clarified and simplified.

In the next example, repetition of *policy regarding the treatment of whistleblowers* unnecessarily lengthens and complicates the sentence. *One* would perform admirably. Rather than write,

> Although EEOC requires no formal policy regarding the treatment of whistleblowers, the CEO wants us to devise a policy regarding the treatment of whistleblowers.

it is much simpler to write,

> Although EEOC requires no formal policy on the treatment of whistleblowers, the CEO wants us to devise one.

In situations where pronouns would be ambiguous or awkward, the good writer finds a synonym made precise by context. For example, *they* in the second sentence below relates (on first reading) to *teams of surgeons.*

> Separate teams of surgeons will perform the operations. They are not life-threatening, and the patient should fully recover within one week.

To avoid indicating that some surgeons (though, mercifully, not these) are life-threatening, the writer substitutes *procedures,* a word that context renders synonymous with *operations.*

Separate teams of surgeons will perform the operations. The procedures are not life-threatening, and the patient should fully recover
within one week.

The same must be said of verbs. Find the precise family of verbs and
remain in that family. If you intend to *change* a clause in a contract, you
can easily shift to *modify* or to *alter*, but *change* is not a synonym for
expand, limit, clarify, or *simplify*. The latter four are far more precise than
change.

In the following paragraph from a trip report, *toured* is unnecessarily
repeated.

On 21 October, we toured Complex 17, where the boosters are
assembled and mated. We then toured Complex 24, the Atlas/
Centaur launch complex. We also toured the Vehicle Assembly
Building, where we observed the movable launcher. We ended the
day by touring the Test Range and Receiving Station.

Toured does not deserve repetition because the reader already infers
the fact. Because the reader infers it, the word is distracting. Some
writers would vary *toured*, substituting *visited, saw, examined,* or *in-
spected*—not a good idea, since these differ substantially from *touring*.
Variation here could easily backfire. After all, when the reader reads *We
saw Complex 24*, he cannot be expected to know that the writer toured it.
In cases like this, when one precise verb applies to a number of events,
use a list:

On 21 October, we toured the following facilities:

• Complex 17, where the boosters are assembled and mated
• Complex 24, the Atlas/Centaur launch complex
• Vehicle Assembly Building
• Test Range and Receiving Station

Words that aren't important enough to deserve an encore should
not receive an encore. Unless you intend to hammer home a logical
argument, vary the "coherence" words. Readers do not lose track of
what you're talking about when you shift from *because* to *since*; they can
easily follow the ideas when you shift from *but* to *however*, or from *also* to
in addition, moreover, and *furthermore*.

Despite the FTC's warning, and regardless of the threat to children's safety, they continued to market the toy. Moreover, they actually increased their advertising during Saturday-morning children's programming. Furthermore, they cut the price of the toy to boost sales.

Because his brain was severely damaged, Dr. Grim decided to operate at once. His patient, Mr. Perdu, was impatient to get on with the procedure, since his brain was damaged too.*

28 Elaborate only when necessary.

A good writer always explains things that require explaining; he will elaborate a point to clarify it, but he will not belabor it.

The distinction between enough and too much is often subtle. When in doubt as to whether readers need information to understand or accept an idea, the writer should provide that information. But when the point can be made clearly and unequivocally in a simple sentence, then added qualifiers and paraphrases not only complicate reading but can actually backfire.

It is vigorously stipulated, upon pain of punishment eternal and everlasting in fire, brimstone, and ice, that the taking of another life by any means whatsoever, be they violent or nonviolent, for any motives whatsoever, be they just or unjust, reasonable or unreasonable, selfish or unselfish, merciful or unmerciful, be the taking premeditated or unpremeditated, and be the victim deserving of being separated from his life or undeserving of said separation, is strictly prohibited.

That sentence, which will look all too familiar to readers of mortgage contracts, insurance policies, retirement plans, loan agreements—in short, to everyone—is an extravagant way of saying, "Thou shalt not kill." The writer has explained too much. *Thou shalt not kill* is clear, simple to understand, and easy to remember; more to the point, it leaves no room for dispute. The legal-sounding version is not only much more difficult to follow—with all of its qualifying phrases, it actually begs readers to find loopholes. When you can make a general statement, make it.

---

*It's not every day that a brain-damaged surgeon performs an operation. Readers will be reassured to know that Mr. Perdu survived this harrowing experience and is recovering nicely.

In the practical world, it is better to write,

Beginning January 1, smoking must be confined to Room 901.

than to write,

Beginning on January 1, the smoking of tobacco products is prohibited in all common areas (meeting rooms, hallways, restrooms, lounges, the cafeteria, and stairwells) and private offices. Those wishing to engage in the smoking of tobacco products may do so in Room 901, a former storage closet. This policy will be in effect for an indefinite period of time.

In the practical world, it is better to write,

Please submit your proposal by April 10.

than to write,

Please ensure that this office receives your proposal to provide the aforementioned service by the date of and not later than April 10.

Writers who believe that the long versions "sound" better need to remember what's written on the STOP sign. Don't explain too much.

29 **Punctuate for nuance, not merely for clarity.**

While anything resembling a comprehensive review of punctuation is outside the scope of this short book, a few words about nuance are essential. Certain marks suggest subtle shades of meaning; the good writer knows when to employ them.

Parenthetical Expressions

In the following sentence, *reversing his position* is parenthetical:

The president, reversing his position, yesterday decided to extend unemployment benefits.

Any phrase is parenthetical when it can be cut from the sentence without changing the writer's intended meaning. Most writers know that these nonessential phrases must be punctuated—but most writers, unfortunately, toss a pair of commas onto the page without pausing to consider that commas may not convey the relative importance of the phrase. Commas do a good job of logically separating a phrase (that's their job), but they cannot suggest nuances that are significant to the writer. Only the writer knows how much emphasis an idea deserves.

Parentheses suggest decreased importance:

The president (reversing his position) yesterday decided to extend unemployment benefits.

Dashes suggest increased importance:

The president—reversing his position—yesterday decided to extend unemployment benefits.

Let's dispose of some superstitions. Many people have been taught that it's "improper" to use parentheses and dashes in formal writing. Teachers say things like, "If you'd put it in parentheses, then it isn't important enough to include, so why say it? Just use commas" and "Dashes make things too lively! Business writing should be more sedate. Just use commas." Such arguments, which deprive the writer of two useful tools, are tantamount to insisting that the sky is blue. Yes, it is blue, of course it is blue, but it is also a hundred differing shades of blue, and every good painter knows it.

Isn't it true that some ideas—even though they are nonessential— are more important than others? Isn't it true that other parenthetical ideas are little more than "Oh, and by the way" sorts of helpful information? Finally, isn't it true that the reader reads what the writer writes? The good writer selects punctuation that reveals subtle shades of importance. Don't vary the marks without reason; know what each suggests, and use them to temper the reader's understanding.

Relationships Between Sentences

Use good judgment when punctuating between sentences. The right mark will reveal the precise relationship, which in turn fosters coherence and simplifies understanding. Many different marks will be "correct," but only one will indicate the sense you wish to convey.

Use a period when each sentence has its own integrity and should be regarded as an independent idea. In the expressions below, semicolons would dilute the emphasis on each separate thought. The period strengthens emphasis.

Thank you for your letter. We are gratified to hear that you're delighted with our product.

Analysis of the photographs reveals nothing conclusive. The tarpaulin-covered objects on the dock at Vladivostok could be anything from weapons to food.

Use a colon when the second sentence summarizes the first. In the examples below, the question "And what was that?" haunts the space between sentences.

> The research proved only one thing: Artificial intelligence remains "artificial."

> The dictator learned something important: Brutality does not work.

Use a dash when the second sentence summarizes the first and deserves special emphasis. Again, you decide what level of emphasis is appropriate. Do you want the reader to pay particular attention to the concluding idea?

> European sales have skyrocketed—revenue is up 25 percent compared to the same quarter one year ago.

> The economists' rosy predictions were wrong—unemployment increased, and the recession deepened.

Use parentheses around the second sentence when you wish to decrease the sense of its importance. Parentheses confer the sense of "Reader, here's a minor point" to an expression (and they are the only marks that do so).

> We have not received payment. (It was due on February 15.)

> Beginning on the first of next month, use the Times Roman font for all customer correspondence. (The font will be loaded into your printers next week.)

Use a semicolon between sentences when (1) neither of the ideas is important enough to stand as a sentence by itself or (2) the ideas are parallel.

> Exempt employees favor the plan; nonexempt employees oppose it.

> The stock market reacted perversely to the terrible earnings report. Ford stock rose two points on the news; GM stock soared four points.

> Skill with language is essential. The quitchweed seed will produce quitchweed; it cannot give rise to an oak. But one's assumptions about communication are important too: Planted in concrete, no seed will grow.

ⒸⒸ **Do not allow dogmatic folderol to interfere with plain style.**

Do not let nonsense parading as "rules" interfere with clarity and simplicity. This language of ours is a wonderful instrument, capable of infinite precision and subtlety. But merely that—merely capable. Writers who tread in the minefield of "don'ts" (e.g., Don't split an infinitive, Don't end a sentence with a preposition, Don't repeat words, Don't let inanimate objects do things) will find needless complexity exploding at every step.

In the United States, there is no consistency in the way English is taught. Teachers disagree about what usages are "proper" and "improper." In seventh grade, Johnny learns never to start a sentence with *because*; in eighth grade, he learns it's okay to start a sentence with *because*, but never ever to start with *so*. In high school, he learns never to use parentheses; in college, he learns never to use dashes, but to use parentheses. At work, his manager (who attended the same college but had a different instructor for Composition 101) insists that parentheses are never necessary, that *contact* isn't a verb, and that *however* must always be followed by a comma.

It's hardly surprising that Johnny (now John) lacks confidence and hates to write. So does his manager. So does the executive vice president. Everyone has been subjected to a chaos of contradictory rights and wrongs, goods and bads, propers and impropers. Sometimes it's miraculous that anything gets written at all.

We live, alas, in an imperfect world, and there will always be readers who snort with righteous annoyance when they spot a split infinitive or a sentence fragment. Some readers will snort about exclamation points; others will snort about single-sentence paragraphs. Any reader who is a diehard pedant will find *something* to snort at. You never know what will make a reader snort, so it's best not to worry about it. We must let these readers snort. Nothing good comes of humoring them. The majority of readers wish merely to understand.

Here is where our thinking should begin: In business, practical communication is what counts. The question is not what Sister Louise said twenty-five years ago, or what Miss Thompson said in ninth grade, or what Assistant Professor Jones said in freshman composition class. The question is this: What works?

③① **Split the infinitive when emphasis requires it.**

If the masters of fashion insisted that gray hats were "incorrect," some people would memorize the "rule," take pains to observe it, and mercilessly berate anyone so incorrect as to wear a gray hat. The practical fellow interested in keeping his head dry will laugh at such silliness.

"Never split an infinitive" is just as silly and as arbitrary. It is not a matter of style but merely one of fashion. No one knows how this baseless convention began, much less how it fossilized into a "rule," but it continues to appear in corporate style guides and textbooks of English. No one knows why. Not only does it needlessly clutter a writer's thinking, but it also frequently obstructs her saying what she means.

When Miss Purselips told us, in seventh grade, that we weren't to split an infinitive, we all agreed that it was horrible to do so and promised we never would. Miss Purselips, bless her soul, knew that we were incapable of using good judgment; she didn't say to us, "Don't put so many words between the *to* and the verb that you rupture continuity." That's what she meant, but she couldn't put it that way because we didn't know what *continuity* was.

Let's reason this through. An infinitive is a *to* with a verb after it, as in *to see* and *to become*. And if the phrase *to thoroughly become disgusted* is bad writing, then it is bad writing only because the writer wished to indicate a *thorough disgust*. In that case, *thoroughly* is in the wrong place; in that case, the phrase should read *to become thoroughly disgusted*. In this instance, the "wrong place" happens to be between a *to* and a verb. But *thoroughly* is also in the wrong place in this sentence: *The state trooper scolded me for driving too fast thoroughly*. (The truth is that he *thoroughly scolded* me.) From this instance, should we generalize and say one can never end a sentence with an adverb?

Put the modifiers where they seem the most natural. Just ensure that they are describing the right thing. Remember the commonsense rule about modifiers: They should appear right beside the word you intend them to describe.

In its fitting rooms, a department store in Chevy Chase, Maryland, prominently displays the following admonition:

> Our policy is to fully prosecute shoplifters.

Here the infinitive is split, and with very good reason. *Fully* modifies *prosecute*, as it should. The sentence is emphatic. But observe how emphasis is crippled when *fully* is moved:

> Our policy is fully to prosecute shoplifters.
>
> Our policy is to prosecute shoplifters fully.

Only a pedant would argue that one of those is in any way "more correct" than the original; only someone who doesn't understand how communication works would maintain that the sentence could read, *Our policy is to prosecute fully shoplifters.* Such an order of words is alien to plain English.

Let's look at additional instances where not splitting the infinitive would be poor judgment. If one has already been assessing a situation, but the assessment has not been done realistically and one wishes to make that point, one writes, for the necessary emphasis,

> To realistically assess the situation, we must visit the site.

If one has already attempted to distinguish the views of two candidates, but no clear distinction has been drawn, one writes, for the appropriate emphasis,

> To clearly distinguish the candidates' views, we need arrange a debate.

One could write, *To draw clear distinctions between* or *To distinguish clearly the candidates' views.* But the first is wordy and unemphatic; the second is awkward because it does not conform to everyday syntax.

CIA's very fine *Style Manual & Writers Guide for Intelligence Publications*, which was written by people fiercely impatient with folderol, puts the matter this way:

> These days, only a pedant would lead a crusade against all split infinitives. So, split when you must, but make sure that clarity or the flow of the sentence demand the split. If you are not sure, do not split.

EPA's *Be a Better Writer: A Manual for EPA Employees* also takes the practical view:

> The tasteful solution [to the problem of whether to split] is to split the infinitive only after you have considered the alternative.

You have judgment. Use it. Isn't it true that of the sentences below, the first does the best job of relating *blithely* to *ignore*?

> To blithely ignore common sense is to invite complexity.
>
> Blithely to ignore common sense is to invite complexity.
>
> To ignore common sense blithely is to invite complexity.

Isn't it true that of the sentences that follow, the first does the best job of relating *radically* to *reduce*?

They have decided to radically reduce fringe benefits.

They have decided radically to reduce fringe benefits.

They have decided to reduce fringe benefits radically.

And isn't it true that of the sentences below, the first does the best job of relating *flatly* to *deny*?

It makes no sense to flatly deny the possibility.

It makes no sense flatly to deny the possibility.

It makes no sense to deny the possibility flatly.

32 Don't breed monsters in the attempt to avoid ending a sentence with a preposition.

Monster, as used here, means "an expression that no one in his right mind would say." Here is a monster:

We finally decided to uplook the definition.

Here is another:

Here is the report for which you asked in which third-quarter costs are analyzed.

The speaker says, "Read what you've written aloud"; the writer writes, "Read aloud what you've written." This is, good advice. If what you've written doesn't sound like something you'd say, then express the idea in a different way. In the ordinary course of a day, would you actually speak the following sentence?

The reporter's arrogance is the thing up with which we cannot put.

Some people might actually say that. Some listeners might simply hear it and not think it sounded ludicrous. Most listeners would wonder whether the speaker learned his English at the University of the Moon. Ordinary speech would cast the expression this way:

The reporter's arrogance is the thing we can't put up with.

That is the way an ordinary speaker of English would say it if he were not on some artificial "grammar alert" or under some other warping influence. Will a good writer write it that way? No.

A good writer will avoid ending a sentence with a preposition for two practical reasons. First, many readers think that such a usage is "wrong." Whether they are correct or incorrect on the point is irrelevant; if they spot the usage, they will wonder about the writer's education and attentiveness to detail. They will cease reading and start editing, which is not what the writer wishes them to do. Second, sentences that end in "phrasal verbs" (*put up with, talked about, heard from,* and so on) are imprecise. The simple solution is to find the one-word verb:

> The reporter's arrogance is the thing we cannot tolerate.

The one-word verb is used in the revisions shown on the right.

Your suggestion has been carefully thought about.	Your suggestion has been carefully considered.
The missing files have not been accounted for.	The missing files have not been located.
Here is the material you asked for.	Here is the material you requested.
The options are worth talking about.	The options are worth discussing.
Several issues need to be called attention to.	Several issues need to be emphasized.
She is the only applicant we have not heard from.	She is the only applicant who has not responded.

33 Use the idiom.

People who view Andy Warhol's painting of a huge can of Campbell's tomato soup are right to pay vigorous attention to that can. Art deserves attention. But people who want to eat Campbell's tomato soup behave differently. They reach into the cupboard, grab the can, open it, get the soup out, and toss the can into the recycling bin. The can is merely functional; very little attention is paid to it.

People read business documents with the same sort of practicality. They read merely for the ideas. Unless style intrudes, they do not notice it; one might say they merely get the soup out of it. In other words, when they read *Appendix B further discusses this issue,* they are not stupefied and do not gasp. They know that Appendix B doesn't talk; more important, they do not understand the sentence to mean that Appendix B might talk. The soup, in this case, is something on the order of, "If you want more information on this issue, look in Appendix B."

Such expressions as *Appendix B discusses, Figure 1 illustrates,* and *this report explains* are called idiomatic (i.e., their practical meaning differs from their literal meaning). Everyone agrees that Figure 1 is inert and doesn't literally illustrate anything; we all agree that a report is really nothing but a stack of pages and can't literally explain anything. But we say that they do, and the reader effortlessly understands us. To insist that a person should never write such expressions as *the results imply* or *the audit revealed* is to mistake how the human mind truly behaves. Business writing isn't art and doesn't receive exquisite scrutiny.

In a nutshell, the issue centers on the writer's choice of a verb. Is it reasonable to say that abstractions and inanimate objects can act? That depends entirely on what we claim the subject is doing. Words present images, and readers may, with justice, bare their teeth at such distracting and bizarre images as these:

> If implemented, the new policy will hairball productivity.
>
> The customer's remark kissed the account manager on the lips.
>
> The corporate dress code disembowels our rights.
>
> The software loudly proclaims that it can catch errors in grammar.

Good judgment is all. The key is to avoid stretching beyond the tolerance of ordinary usage. There is a vast difference, after all, between the simple, unobtrusive *The deadline is creeping up on us* and the strange, attention-grabbing *The deadline is slithering up on us*. The latter sentence certainly has a lair somewhere under the Northern Lights, but it is out of place in a rational climate. So are the following sentences in the left column.

With a word, his memo parted the stormy Red Sea of confusion engulfing the policy.	His memo clarified the policy.
Your invoice is snoring peacefully on the vice president's desk.	Your invoice remains on the vice president' desk.
The results of the survey goosed the CEO into action.	Alarmed at the results of the survey, the CEO took action.

Writers who wish to create poems should certainly do so; each poem improves the world. But those writers are encouraged to write poems at home, not at work. In the realm of business writing, at least, the reader is not prey. No verb should ambush him.

With that caveat in mind, the practical writer will freely use everyday expressions to simplify things for the reader. Note how conciseness and emphasis improve in the examples on the right when the idiom replaces the "literal" language in the sentences on the left.

It is implied in this advertising that the interest rate is fixed.	This advertising implies that the interest rate is fixed.
An exploration of the relationship between literacy and income is presented in this short report.	This short report explores the relationship between literacy and income.
This strategy may have an effect opposite to the one intended.	This strategy may backfire.
The new policy should result in a pronounced positive effect on sales.	The new policy should boost sales.
Representatives of the company claim that the sanctions are biased and unfair.	The company claims that the sanctions are biased and unfair.
His second article contains an elaboration of the issue.	His second article elaborates the issue.
In the Preface, the writer presents justification for the method used in the research.	The Preface justifies the method used in the research.
Their conclusions are certainly deserving of serious consideration.	Their conclusions demand serious consideration.
These results are based on the assumption that people are candid in their response to the survey.	These results assume that people respond honestly to the survey.
In the Introduction is presented a strong case for permitting employees to fire their managers.	The Introduction presents a strong case for permitting employees to fire their managers.
The finding was made of several serious discrepancies in the audit.	The audit found several serious discrepancies.
This confusion provides proof that the translation is inaccurate.	This confusion proves that the translation is inaccurate.
As a result of the new campaign, sales have increased an impressive extent.	As a result of the new campaign, sales have skyrocketed.
Typos will be found when the writer fails to pay adequate attention to the text.	Typos lurk where an inattentive writer has been.

⟨34⟩ Use personal pronouns when they are necessary.

Many writers learn that personal pronouns (*I, you, we,* and so forth) are inappropriate in business and technical writing. A common argument is that personal pronouns make writing "informal." What we have in this argument is the failure to distinguish between "informal" and "personal." And this isn't a matter of mere semantics. The difference is tremendous, and the failure to respect that difference will result in complex writing.

All of the sentences below are "formal" English (i.e., they conform to the agreed-upon standards of "correctness").

It is the opinion of this writer that the proposal should be accepted.	I believe that we should accept the proposal.
Should there be any questions about the scope of work, please direct abovementioned questions to the undersigned.	If you have any questions about the scope of work, please direct them to me.

All of those are "formal." The two on the left are impersonal; the two on the right are personal. But that is an academic distinction. What is the practical distinction? Isn't it true that you find the sentences on the right easier to understand? Furthermore, isn't it true that you are not fooled by the artifice in the sentences on the left?

The reader isn't fooled when she encounters an expression like *this office is of the belief that*. She rummages around in those words and comes up with the sense of "we believe." She isn't hoodwinked by *the author of this report*; she delves beneath the phrase and unearths the shy "I." In plain style, the word for *I* is *I* and nothing else, not *this writer, this observer, this reporter, this researcher, this analyst,* the lunatic *this desk,* or the maniacal *the undersigned*.

People hear things like, "Don't use *I* because using that word suggests that you're too important." But that's true only when *I* is repeated inappropriately. In the short paragraph below, the writer is clearly calling attention to herself. If that's her intention, then she's done a good job conveying it.

> I have concluded my research, and I believe that I have discovered a new way to predict customers' behavior. I have used the multivariate model, and I am confident that my results are accurate.

If, on the other hand, the writer herself is less important than the research, then the repeated *I* is inappropriate—not wrong, not improper, not informal—merely inappropriate. Remember Technique 8: Put the right word first and tell the truth. If the writer intends to emphasize the research, then *research* becomes the subject, and her good judgment would cast the ideas like this:

The research strongly indicates a new (and more reliable) approach to predicting customers' behavior. The multivariate model was used to ensure the accuracy of the results.

35 Use one-sentence paragraphs for emphasis.

"A paragraph must contain more than one sentence" makes excellent sense in seventh grade, when we are first learning how to write a topic sentence and use transitional phrases. But we aren't in seventh grade anymore, and we can't afford to be trapped in seventh-grade reasoning.

Remember: The first principle of emphasis is isolation.

You isolate an idea to emphasize it. Short sentences have punch. Longer ones, such as the one you're reading now, dilute emphasis because each idea clamors for equal attention. The technique of isolation works for paragraphs as it does for sentences; the only thing you need to consider is how much emphasis an idea deserves. If you want the reader to pay particular attention to a sentence, give that sentence a paragraph to itself.

Your job is to direct the reader's understanding—his understanding not only of your intended meaning, but also of the relative importance of phrases and sentences. The reader is incapable of clairvoyance and relies on you to tell him when one sentence deserves particular stress. And one very good way to stress a sentence is to give it "paragraph weight."

Just remember that effect diminishes with repetition. When the reader encounters a page where every sentence is a paragraph, the technique is useless. What matters here is contrast, so use the one-sentence-paragraph technique in contrast to your regular paragraphs (where you discuss a topic at some length).

Tip: One excellent place for a single-sentence paragraph is at the beginning of any document. Readers pay particular attention to opening statements. Just make sure that the opening sentence provides a strong focus. Below is an example of this technique.

On the first of next month, your medical insurance benefits will change.

On that date, we will convert to an HMO. We emphasize that you remain fully covered and that your annual maximum for out-of-pocket expenses is still $250.

The new coverage will differ from the old only in one respect: You will be asked to select a physician from among those who are participating in the HMO. We regret that you will no longer be able to visit your favorite doctor, but the 250 physicians participating in our HMO are capable professionals, and we believe that you will easily find one you respect and trust.

We decided to convert to the HMO after receiving our current provider's notice of a fee increase. Our costs and your out-of-pocket maximums would have tripled this year. Within the next week, you will be receiving information about our new coverage. Please contact Ulfin Smith in Benefits Administration if you have any questions about our new medical plan.

36 **Shift tenses when the truth demands it.**

"You must never shift tenses" is another bit of dogma that creates needless confusion. Tenses often must shift; merely avoid changing from one to the other without justification. Clearly, it makes no sense to write something like *We toured Complex 17, where we see how the boosters are assembled*—there's no reason to shift from past to present there—but few professionals are likely to write something like that.

In business writing, the mischief occurs not because people shift tenses when they shouldn't, but because they fail to shift tenses when they should. And most of the confusion involves the use of the "simple present" tense. This is the tense we use to state that a thing is perpetually true (or that we believe it to be true):

> Absence makes the heart grow fonder.
>
> The earth orbits the sun.
>
> Tax incentives stimulate economic activity.
>
> Good writing is good business.

When a thing is over and done with, we put it in the past tense (e.g., *NASA launched the* Voyager *spacecraft many years ago*), but when a thing is true now, we state it in the present (e.g., Voyager *continues to transmit data*). Thus, the following sentence tells the truth:

> *Voyager*, launched many years ago, continues to transmit data.

That sentence will look perfectly fine to most people. But what about this one?

> Even 2,000 years ago, the Greeks suspected that matter is composed of atoms.

Many professionals would write *was composed* in that sentence. But *matter was composed of atoms* is untrue—or at least it is if you believe in the atomic theory. The Greeks' suspecting is done, but what they suspected is held to be a fact, and the tense must shift to the simple present to indicate this.

In precisely the same fashion, we must change from past to present in cases where we are distinguishing the fact that we *did* something from what the results *are*. Note the difference in meaning in the following examples.

[If members no longer prefer hosted tours, or if the validity of the finding is in doubt.]

We conducted focus groups and discovered that our members preferred hosted tours to escorted tours.

[If "members prefer hosted tours" is a finding presumed to be valid.]

We conducted focus groups and discovered that our members prefer hosted tours to escorted tours.

[If the validity of the research is in doubt, or if the labeling has been simplified.]

The research, completed last year, strongly indicated that people were confused by the labeling.

[If the research is accurate, and people remain confused by the labeling.]

The research, completed last year, strongly indicates that people are confused by the labeling.

On Choosing Words

In a single sentence, Ben Franklin summed up the wisdom involved in choosing words. He didn't write, "Lexical decisions resulting in the arcane are decidedly inferior to aforesaid decisions resulting in the mundane." He could have written it that way (he certainly knew all those words), but he didn't. Ben was a clear thinker, and he knew that unusual words obstruct understanding. Because he wanted people to understand him, he wrote, "Never use a longer word when a shorter word will do."

The good writer won't quibble with that. He won't fiddle with the definition of *shorter* and pretend that since *nexus* has only two syllables, it's a short-enough word. If he's writing to a general audience, he'll use *link*. He won't pump helium into his link and release it to waft into the reader's mind as *linkage*. He'll use *link*.

He'll use *link* as a verb or a noun, depending on what he chooses to emphasize. He might write, for example, "How are the two issues linked?" He might write, "I see no link between the two issues." But he'd never use *linkage* as a verb, committing something like, "We must linkage the issues." And he would never, unless he wishes to amuse himself, use *nexus* as a verb, which would result in a sentence like "Diplomats from the two countries are attempting to nexus the issues." He won't clap a verb-sounding ending onto *nexus* and come up with *nexify* or *nexusize*. He's a good writer, not a nitwit. He'll use *link*.

What's interesting about Franklin's remark is that it's phrased as an edict. Ben didn't bother to explain why shorter words are better than longer ones because he assumed that the common sense in his remark is self-evident. But Franklin was a child of the Enlightenment, and he believed that Reason would always be recognized as such. It isn't.

When we scorn little words—when everyday words don't seem "good enough"—we open the door to complexity and sometimes to disaster. A writer at a federal agency, wishing to describe a professional position, meant to say, "This position requires MC&G certification." He could have used those words, but he did not. He reversed Franklin's axiom and didn't use a shorter word when he could hallucinate a longer one, and this is what he wrote:

This position is encumbered by a qualified MC&G professional.

It's easy to trace what happened here. The writer knew something (but not nearly enough) about the word *incumbent*, tried to make a verb of it, misspelled it, and ended up with *encumbered*. He wrote a clear sentence that is not remotely related to what he meant. And he did this because, to him, ordinary words were "unprofessional."

Plain style begins here: The words we use must never impose an artificial complexity on an idea. "Artificial" is the key. Things are complicated enough without our creating a veneer of needless complication. The beauty of accepting this is that it gives us freedom to write simply: *Combat emplacement evacuator* reverts to *shovel* and *taking a proactive position* reverts to *act*. If a writer does not accept it—if he insists on using *utilize* where the sense is simply *use*—then plain style stands no chance. Don't open the door to complexity. It's always out there, snorting and pawing the ground, waiting for its moment in the china shop.

Nowhere in this book will you find *ameliorate* used in battle, though *improve* is used a lot. Nowhere in this book will you find *elucidate* doing the work of *clarify*. I respect your intelligence, and I believe that you know the longer words, but I also believe that *clarify* is clearer on first reading than *elucidate*. I believe that the distinction between *ameliorate* and *improve* is so minor that it makes no sense to use *ameliorate*. I think I would be a bad writer if I wrote something like, *To ameliorate your writing, elucidate the relationships between periodic expressions*. That's inflated style. What I want to say is complicated enough—and because that's so, you benefit when I write it this way: *To improve your writing, clarify the relationships between sentences*. That's plain style.

Maybe you've noticed that those frightening "English teacher" words—*gerund, participle, correlative conjunction, subjunctive, imperative*, and so on—appear nowhere in this book. If I know my audience, those terms are impractical: Not only do they fail to convey anything, but they provoke nightmarish associations and memories. I know that your eyes would glaze if I wrote something like, *A coordinating conjunction is preceded by a comma when it connects independent clauses*. Mine would glaze if I had to read something like that. And it seems to me that glazed eyes signal bad writing.

The elucidation of one's intention has its locus in the selection of the elements of diction is an eye-glazing way of saying, in plain style, *Clarity starts with the choice of words*. Give yourself permission to use ordinary words. Clarity will follow.

How to Find the Right Words

People frequently complain that they have trouble finding the words for an idea. Everyone who's ever tried to write has experienced the same difficulty: "I know what I mean, but I can't seem to put it on paper."

This trouble stems from one (or more) of three sources. First, it's quite possible that we *don't* know what we mean. The idea may not be a clear one after all—we never know whether any idea is clear until we see it on the page, and we might need to concentrate a bit more or examine the rough idea from several angles before the thought itself crystallizes for us. Second, we may be able to *sense* the right words but be unable to call them forth; they tease and tantalize in the back of the mind, flirting with the forebrain but refusing to reveal themselves. This is a matter of our employing those words infrequently, so that they're not part of the "active" vocabulary. To overcome this problem, all that is necessary is a larger vocabulary, a facility with words. Finally, we sometimes simply don't like the way a clear idea sounds. This is a dark impulse, the ogre in the writer's spirit. It is a matter not of having little facility with words, but of having little respect for them and little concern for the reader. The ogre snares a perfectly lucid expression like *As we agreed, the contract amount has been increased by $100,000* and "professionalizes" it into *Per agreement, subject contract funding terms have been adjusted upward in an amount not to exceed $100,000.*

The ogre vanishes in a little puff of smoke when you butt him with a hard head. That happens somewhere on the mystic plane. In the tangible world, the other two difficulties in finding words can be overcome with practice. Here are some suggestions:

■ *Develop a practical vocabulary.* Note the word *practical*. While nothing's wrong with having *arride* and *nuque* in your vocabulary, when will you ever have occasion to use them outside a game of Scrabble or a crossword puzzle? It makes much more sense to know the shades of meanings of everyday words.

Consider the varieties of *looking*. A scientist *observes*, an editor *scrutinizes*, EPA *monitors*, FBI and CIA *surveille*, an angry person *glares*, a surprised person *stares*, a very surprised person *gapes*, and a person beyond gaping *gawks*. We *watch, ogle, gaze, view, review, oversee, rubberneck, leer, squint, admire, glance, overlook, glimpse, peer,* and *peek*—and all these words convey something different. A crop can be in some way damaged, or it can be *stunted, withered, wilted,* or *shriveled;* a policy can positively affect sales, or it can *buoy, increase, boost,* or *stimulate* them. Must you write *initiate*? Are you truly *initiating,* or actually *beginning* or *starting?* And even if professionals in your field use *initiate* to describe the precise origination of something, will the reader of *this* sentence partake of the same distinction? If all the reader wants to know is when something began, then *began* will do perfectly well, and *initiate* will be excessive. Collect and use the practical words.

▪ *Know the meanings of the words you use every day.* If you do, you'll use *utilize* only when you've been ingenious in your use of something (you might utilize this book as a doorstop, for example). You'll use *expect* when an outcome is definite (a pregnant woman expects a baby); you'll use *anticipate* when the outcome is less definite (she anticipates the date of birth).

Respecting the precise definitions of words enables the writer to convey subtle distinctions and shades of meaning. Not respecting them creates confusion, but it enables the writer to show off. For people who wish to show off, every *repetitive* becomes a *redundant*, every *define* becomes a *definitize*, and every *unclear* becomes an *ambiguous*. What some writers fail to recognize is that the longer words are not precise synonyms for the shorter ones.

Ambiguous, for example, is not necessarily a synonym for *unclear*. *Ambiguous* has a precise meaning and denotes a particular problem with clarity (that an expression has two or more logical meanings); *unclear* might mean merely "vague," but it could mean "confusing," "muddled," "cloudy," "murky," or even "deceptive." And for every *unclear* that erroneously becomes an *ambiguous*, we have an *outline* puffing up into a *delineation*, a *fire* exploding into a *conflagration*, a simple *method* ballooning into a *methodology*, and a *granting immunity* whooping into an *immunize*. (This enables us to immunize witnesses without breaking the skin.)

Learn the shades of distinction inherent in the words of everyday writing—the difference between *delay* and *postpone*, the difference between *we have often requested* and *we have repeatedly requested*, the difference between *we anxiously await your response* and *we eagerly await your response*. The everyday words are the practical words to know.

▪ *Read.* Writers who rarely read cannot reasonably expect to develop a sense of the nuances of words. You do not need to read voraciously, or even every day, but you do need to read—a newspaper, a magazine article, a novel, *something* other than the memos and reports that lurch through the halls of business and government. What's important to understand is that "organizational" writing tends to inbreed, with the same results as those when people inbreed: Certain traits, not always good ones, become exaggerated.

Read with a critical eye. When do good writers use *leave?* When do they use *depart*? When do they use *proportion*, and when *percentage*? You'll learn that *likely* is most often used as an adjective (an outcome is likely) and that *probably* is an adverb (something will probably happen). You'll notice that there is a world of difference between *enable* and *allow*, between *prohibit* and *forbid*, between *if* and *whether*. In a good newspaper, you'll find *insure* used only in the context of insurance, *assure* used when the sense is person-to-person (the CEO assured the stockholders of something), and *ensure* for every other sense of "make certain" (we need to ensure that our product is safe). Such distinctions are the ones worth knowing, and you'll learn them if you read. Watch your source; read well-written material. A supermarket tabloid may do more harm than good.

- *Visualize.* Use your imagination to "see" the action. If you want to indicate that two wires should be connected and made into one, you could use *attach together* or *connect together*, but if you visualize it, you'll find *splice*. If you remember and visualize a time when you *did not bother to*, you'll find *neglected*; if you visualize a time when you *did not take something into consideration*, you'll find *overlooked*, *disregarded*, or *ignored*. Visualize it. Are you *attaching* or merely *enclosing* something? Did the executives truly *discuss* the contract, or did they *debate* or *argue* about it? Did they *squabble, bicker, dispute*? Which word best captures the truth? When employees have paper to recycle, do they put it into a *container*, or into a *box*, a *bin*, a *tray*, or a *can*? Is this document a *contract*, a *proposal*, a *memo*, an *analysis*, a *report*, an *article*, a *pamphlet*, a *brochure*, an *announcement*, a *newsletter*, an *invoice*, or a *monograph*?

- *Demand precision from yourself.* When we write about concrete things—about bricks, trucks, and butterfly bolts—conveying ideas is difficult enough. Unfortunately, much of business writing is necessarily abstract (we write more about intangible things like *customer satisfaction* and *rule-making procedures* than we do about physical bricks). And in the domain of abstractions, choosing precise words becomes imperative. Call things by their right names.

Select your nouns with care. Is the right word *statute* or *regulation*? Is the right word *policy* or *procedure*? In business, individual customers receive *bills*, and organizations receive *invoices*. Sellers charge a *price*; buyers think in terms of *cost*. Be especially exact in your choice of verbs. A launch can be *delayed*, or it can be *postponed indefinitely, canceled*, or *aborted*. If you demand precision, you'll never write, *The SEC's ruling will impact sales*. Instead, you'll use a precise verb: The ruling will *increase, decrease, complicate, jeopardize, boost, cripple, stimulate, simplify, ensure*, or do something else in particular to sales.

- *Trust yourself.* If the sense you wish to convey is "Opening an office in San Diego would be impractical," then go ahead and write that. Why look for another way to put it? If you look for a "better" way to say it, the sentence will inflate into something on the order of *At this point in time, the establishment of a San Diego regional facility would not seem to be a prudent or viable goal.* Somewhere in that flurry of syllables is your plain idea; your original words expressed it best. If you want to convey that "Customers are complaining that our bills are difficult to understand," then use those words. They're good ones. Don't pump the idea full of anabolic steroids, so that it reads, *The majority of our clientele have recently voiced discomfort with our invoicing documents, claiming that these documents are difficult to comprehend.* Just write your original sentence. Trust yourself.

If you have a clear thought, chances are 100 percent that it is packaged in clear words. If the idea is clear, all you need to do is give yourself permission to write it that way. In workshops, I sometimes ask writers to pick a word that best captures a sense. I might, for example, ask them to select the best word for the sense of "rare" from the list below:

> rare
> unusual
> strange
> unique
> uncommon

Many writers pause to think about the matter. Some select *strange* or *unique*. I point out that the word for *rare* is *rare*, just as the word for *policy* is *policy* and the word for *must* is *must*. You can't out-think the definitions of words. The eyes light up. Could it truly be that easy? Of course it can! And unless the writer is complicating things, it ought to be just that easy.

We extend this reasoning to entire sentences. Someone at FDA, intending to convey that *Currently, we are unsure whether Aspartame is dangerous*, once wrote, *Aspartame is potentially dangerous.* Most people, aware of how FDA determines whether a substance is dangerous, assume that the sentence means "Aspartame is dangerous if you consume a large amount of it." This is another thought entirely, but it is the one most apparent in that sentence.

I ask writers a simple question: If the writer wishes to let readers know that *Currently, we are unsure whether Aspartame is dangerous*, then what are the words for that thought? "Those words," someone will say. "Those exact words." And she'll be right. False teeth are false teeth, and if Mr. Smith ordered a set of false teeth, then the way to say it is *Mr. Smith ordered a set of false teeth*, not *A full complement of compensated edentia was requisitioned by Mr. Smith.* Writers with a taste for the bizarre and the baroque are encouraged to become diplomats, stand-up comedians, or high-level politicians. Rare words sparkle everywhere in these professions, where the meaning of a statement isn't as important as its immediate effect.

Some Common Problems With Ordinary Words

A number of very good books explain the distinction between pairs of words like *less* and *fewer, insure* and *ensure,* and *whether* and *if.* The words discussed here complicate understanding even though they are "correct." They are listed in order of their potential to create mischief:

- Avoid relying on *affect* or *impact* as verbs. They are correct, but they never convey anything in particular. If you mean that the new software will increase productivity, then don't write, *The new software will affect productivity.* Use *increase* as the verb. If you mean that a report boosted consumers' confidence, then say that. Avoid writing, *The report impacted consumer confidence.* It is wishful thinking to believe that *positively impact* and *negatively impact* are better; they are wordy as well as imprecise. If you mean *stimulate* and *jeopardize,* say so. The reader reads the words, not the mind.

- Avoid *shall,* a notoriously ambiguous word that can indicate either *will* or *must.* In a sentence such as *The contractor shall fully document all indirect costs,* the word *shall* can be interpreted to mean that the contractor intends to (will) document indirect costs or that the contractor is legally obligated to (must) document indirect costs. Writers who mean *must* are strongly encouraged to write *must.* Writers who wish to indicate a future tense are strongly encouraged to write *will.*

- Be careful with *may.* Incautious use of this word leads to ambiguity, as in *The auditors may photocopy all records.* Does this mean that the auditors have authority to photocopy, or that they possibly will photocopy? In the former case, use *are authorized to;* in the latter case, use *might.*

- Use *this, that, these,* and *those* to refer to previously mentioned topics. Substitute them for the horribly intrusive *said, above, abovementioned,* and the grotesque *heretoforeabovementioned.* After you introduce a contract, refer to it as *this contract,* or *the contract,* not *the abovementioned contract.* When you're referring to more than one contract, write *these contracts,* not *said contracts* or *the above contracts.* That's what *this* and *these* are for.

■ In memos, avoid referring to the issue in the SUBJECT line as *subject issue* or *captioned* issue. Doing so interrupts the flow of reading because it yanks the reader back to the top of the page. For example, if the SUBJECT line reads *ODM contract terms*, don't begin the memo with the phrase *Subject contract*. Instead, write a civilized expression: *We need to clarify several terms in our contract with ODM*.

■ Challenge the verb *support*; look instead for the precise verb. *Support* is vague. In *These findings support the conclusion that*, the findings could *indicate, prove, underscore, reveal, imply, verify, confirm, suggest*, or *demonstrate*. In *We can support our sales force by improving customer service*, the meaning is simply *help* or *assist*. When one writes, *The company supports employee participation in*, one could mean that the company *encourages, endorses, funds, simplifies*, or even *mandates*. Challenge this word each time you use it.

■ Beware *potentially*. The word is often redundant, frequently confused with *probably*, and repeatedly misleading when used to indicate a lack of certainty. Taken at face value, *potentially dangerous* and *potentially hazardous* are redundant (*dangerous* and *hazardous* indicate the potential for harm). In *The new advertising is potentially misleading*, the writer intends to indicate either some degree of probability or a lack of certainty. *The new advertising could [might, will probably] mislead our customers* would do in the former case. In the latter case, write, *We are unsure whether the advertising is accurate*.

■ Don't generalize about *-ize* words. A Secretary of Commerce once wrote a memo in which he forcefully admonished his writers never to use any word that ends in *-ize*. This admonition, which stemmed from his frustration with *prioritize*, robbed writers of some very useful words: *Maximize, minimize, sanitize*, and *scrutinize*, for example, are all simple. Writers at Commerce found that they could no longer simply *realize* something but had to *be of the realization that*. Common sense argues that there is a gulf of difference between a common word like *terrorize* and mind-boggling, spur-of-the-moment inventions like *incentivize* ("motivate," "convince," "persuade," "entice," "encourage"), *functionalize* (a hallucinatory word that means "open," "complete," or "prepare"), *orientize* (just say "orient" or "acquaint"), and *diminize* ("reduce" would perform admirably). Our language is leaping with verbs. Find the right one.

■ Avoid transparent, clichéd euphemisms such as *this office, this company*, and *this organization*. When the reference is clear, just write *we*. Sentences such as *This office is in receipt of your letter* are instantly translated into *We have received your letter*. The reader should not need to translate her own language. When you need to say *I*, don't write, *this writer, this office, this desk, this author,* or any other phony substitute. Write *I.* That's what the word is for. Anything else is needless complication.

▪ Whenever possible, avoid euphemisms. Most euphemisms suggest bad faith. The famous *unintended impact with the ground* (airplane crash), *revenue enhancements* (tax increases), and *collateral damage* (damage to nonmilitary targets in war) spring from the writer's belief that he can cloak an unpleasant truth in vague or abstract words. This practice backfires. Readers are not fooled for long, and when they grasp the plain meaning, they realize the writer's attempt to deceive.

▪ Minimize your use of "legal-sounding" terms. *Heretofore* is a chuckleheaded way to write *previously. Herein* and *herewith* are nearly always redundant (*herein enclosed is* means "enclosed is"). *Pursuant to our discussion* usually means "as we discussed" or "as a follow-up to our discussion." In ordinary English, *henceforth, hereafter,* and *hereinafter* mean "from now on." In plain style, the dwarves *therein* and *wherein* mean nothing more than "there" and "where," respectively. Besides complicating the text, such words destroy tone, rendering the writing mercilessly cold.

▪ Shun archaic words. The word for *two times* is *twice,* but to indicate *three times* you need to write *three times. Thrice* is outmoded and calls attention to itself, just as *beseech* and *behoove* are outmoded and distracting. *It would behoove us to reduce our price* was a grand expression in 1618, but these days *We need to reduce our price* is more effective. *Betwixt and between* may seem like a saucy phrase the first time you hear it, but *between* will suffice. *Wherefore* takes people to the balcony scene in *Romeo and Juliet*—as pleasant interlude, perhaps, but hardly a desirable detour in a contract. Just write *why.* Use reasonable contemporary words.

▪ Use extreme caution when importing foreign words and phrases. Readers might be familiar with *vis-à-vis,* but why take the chance? Use *about* or *regarding.* Only if all of your intended readers know French will *élan* give your sentence a dash of *je ne sais quoi.* Lovely Italian words like *pentimento* and *glissando,* as mellifluous as they are, belong to the arts and are best confined there. If you must discuss *bubei* (a Japanese word meaning "regretful contempt for America"), then define the word when you introduce it. Phrases from Latin are particularly obnoxious to most readers, and writers (including attorneys who write to a general audience) are strongly encouraged to stop baffling the rest of us with such mysterious remarks as *in re, pro se, res ipsa loquitur,* and *inter alia.* The writer may know what these phrases mean, but that is never the point. It's best to write in English.

- Be careful with jargon. Jargon (technical terms unique to a profession) is useful shorthand when it remains within the confines of a specific priesthood. When it escapes those confines—when readers do not belong to the priesthood—it is as incomprehensible as any foreign language. The strangely enticing phrase *charismatic megafauna* means "lions, tigers, and bears" to people at EPA, but *lions, tigers, bears, and other large animals* would prevent most readers from guessing. Telecommunications engineers can bandy *uplinks, downlinks,* and *transponders* back and forth to one another with great success, but the general audience needs those terms defined (a diagram wouldn't hurt). In computerspeak, *an AI application presupposes RAM, datalinks propagate,* and *modules migrate.* Every word has its place, and those are fine in the community of computer experts. But for the general audience they are profanely absurd—just as the English teacher's *imperative indicative* is absurd when it is launched at the tender ears of seventh graders. Readers may not need to encounter the technical terms in order to get on with understanding.

- Use careful judgment when you introduce acronyms and abbreviations. If your readers are familiar with *ATM,* then you needn't clutter the text by formally introducing the abbreviation, as in *For your convenience, we are installing an Automated Teller Machine (ATM).* Common abbreviations require no explanation. Unfamiliar ones do. If your intended readers will not instantly recognize *BARF* to stand for the "Best Available Retrofit Facility," then common courtesy suggests that you spell the name and then introduce the abbreviation. But don't introduce *BARF* merely for the sake of introducing it. When you introduce an abbreviation, do so because you'll need to refer to it at least once more (and fairly soon) in the document. Unless you have occasion to use the abbreviation again, introducing it is nothing but clutter. Be alert to wishful thinking. Some accountants believe that *K* means "thousands" and *M* means "millions." Other accountants read *M* as *thousands,* believing that if you meant *millions* you would write *MM.* If you have the least suspicion that the reader may not share your intended meaning for an abbreviation, then specify what you mean by it.

- Know how to use *i.e.* and *e.g.* The device *i.e.* means "that is" or "in other words." Use it to paraphrase, clarify, or point out something about the previous expression, and introduce it with parentheses: *Human error contributed to the accident at Chernobyl (i.e., the technology was only partly to blame).* The device *e.g.* means "for example" and is introduced with parentheses: *Smoking has been banned in many common areas (e.g., hallways, lounges, and the cafeteria).* Writers are forever confusing these devices, and often with serious implications. In *Contractor agrees to replace defaulting items (i.e., fuses and bulbs) for two years from the installation date*, the contractor is liable only for the fuses and the bulbs. The writer intended to supply examples of items, but *i.e.* does not supply examples. It paraphrases what the writer meant by *items*. Practical sense argues that the phrases *for example* and *that is* are good ones to use; they are less likely to be confused.

▪ Be careful with *a* and *an*. The use of *a* and *an* has nothing to do with vowels and consonants. Use *a* before a consonant sound and *an* before a vowel sound. It is *a unique* solution, *a one-time* adjustment, *a European* office; it is *an MX* missile, *an FDIC-insured* account, *an hourly* rate.

▪ Honor connotations. Their product is *cheap*, but ours is *affordable*. They are *timid;* we are *prudent*. They may be *stubborn, inflexible, dogmatic, obstinate, obdurate*, or *muleheaded*, but we are *firm*. Pay attention to the echoes and associations of words. A client can be *late* paying an invoice, or he can be *delinquent*. In most businesses, it's better to *serve* customers than to *service* them.

▪ Don't terrify the reader with *be advised that*. By convention, this phrase is used to introduce something that the reader is not going to like very much: *Be advised that we are investigating allegations concerning your conduct, Be advised that your property taxes will increase, Be advised that the reduction in revenue will necessitate layoffs*. Reserve your use of this phrase for those occasions when the matter is truly serious. When the news is positive or neutral, write, *Please note that* or *Note that* instead.

▪ Beware of unintentionally insulting the reader with *for your information*. The phrase *for your information* has become forever linked with the defensive sense of "You're wrong, pal, and I'm about to straighten things out." When the bank falsely accuses you of failing to pay your mortgage on time, you respond, with justifiable annoyance, "For your information, the check cleared ten days ago." If you do not intend to convey indignation, substitute a precise phrase. *For your information, we are enclosing our brochure* could easily become *The enclosed brochure will acquaint you with our capabilities*. If you wish to indicate that no action is required, use *FYI*. While those letters "stand for" *for your information*, their practical effect is to convey "this is information only."

▪ Beware *obviously*. Numerous relationships have been sunk by this torpedo of a word, which in effect calls the reader a dunce for not knowing what the writer, in his wisdom, already knows. *Obviously, you don't understand the complexities of the research* is degrading in the extreme. *It's obvious that funding this project would be a waste of money* is a bullying statement—the sort people resort to when they have no evidence to support their point and must rely on brawn alone. *The advantages of our product are obvious* will backfire. Words are cheap. Give the reader credit for having some intelligence. Lead her to that conclusion, but allow her to draw it.

▪ Avoid writing like a robot. The thrill of such phrases as *per our telecom, input appreciated,* and *receipt is noted* wears off very quickly for human readers. Plain style requires not that you write precisely as you speak, but that what you write might actually issue from the mouth of a sane, sensible, sober, awake, and reasonably courteous person. If you'd feel strange saying what you've written—if people would look askance at you and take a step away—then what you've written needs to be simplified.

▪ Avoid wrenching nouns into verbs. Rather than *dialogue* with people, it's simpler to *meet, talk,* or *confer* with them. Rather than *reference* something, just *refer* to it. *Memorandum all employees* is a grotesque way of saying *Write a memo to all employees.* Such a sentence as *They informationed us that the tremors had subsided* is a sadly comic way of saying they *told* us or *informed* us. Nouns are very good at being nouns, but they fall woefully short of the stamina required of verbs.

▪ Refrain from coining words. *Unsave* happened one day when a writer couldn't think of another way to say that he intended to *erase, delete,* or *dump* data from a file. *Incent* happened one day when a writer wished to shorten *incentivize,* which occurred one day when another writer couldn't find a way to say *motivate, entice, encourage, persuade,* or *convince.* The inclination to clap an *-ize* onto the backside of a noun is especially strong in bureaucracies: *quantity* becomes *quanticize* ("count"), *liquid* becomes *liquidize* ("melt"), and *arson* becomes *arsonize* (as in *Security now believes that someone arsonized the plant*). Marketing calls are not glorified but merely dandified when they are referred to as marketing *outdials;* calls from customers need not be tarted up into *customer indials.* And while it may seem logical for *prepone* to be the opposite of *postpone,* such a sentence as *Next week's meeting has been preponed to tomorrow* is little more than evidence of a frustrated comedian. Use ordinary words for ordinary things.

▪ When you must name something (e.g., a project, study, or device), give it a clear and logical name. *Functional Illiteracy* is an impressive title for a report, but what does it mean? Is illiteracy in some way functional? Is someone functional even though he's classified as illiterate? Can someone barely function *because* he's illiterate? No one knows. An *Elderly Care Program* has nothing to do with care that is elderly, but is concerned with *Caring for the Elderly.* Don't be brief at the expense of your meaning. A *homeless advocate* is an advocate without a home, just as a *handicapped activist* is an activist who is handicapped. If you mean one who is an advocate for the homeless, say so; if you mean an activist for the handicapped, say so. Referring to boots as *leather personnel carriers* (the Army shortens this to LPCs) and to a telephone as a *telephonic communications instrument* is utter madness. Those things already have names.

- Challenge the everyday jargon of business. *Implement* and *institute* are vague words, sometimes intended as "adopt" and sometimes as "carry out" or "put into practice." In *We implemented the policy last year*, the reader is at sea. *Prioritize* is a hideous word masking the much simpler *rank*, as in *The executives met to discuss and prioritize corporate goals*. Another problem with *prioritize* is that it lays eggs, and what hatches from those eggs are phrases like *performed a prioritization of*. Shiny, newly minted terms are especially seductive and require extra restraint. Like will-o'-the-wisps leading the unwary into quicksand, *build-down*, *negrowth*, and *downsize* have an allure fatal to simplicity and clarity. It is better to dismantle something than to *effect a build-down* of it, better to say that the economy is shrinking than to say it is *experiencing negrowth*, and far more courageous and humane to say *reduce the number of employees* than to say *downsize*.

- Avoid clichés. When phrases are cheapened through too-frequent use, they lose their power to ignite in the reader's imagination. Empty phrases like *state-of-the-art, few and far between*, and *once-in-a-lifetime opportunity* are little more than collections of syllables, husks from which the cicadas have flown. Rubber-stamp expressions such as *We are in receipt of your letter of March 19* and *Feel free to call me if you have any questions* make things easy for the writer—but because the reader encounters them a hundred times a year, they are little more than background noise. Those sentences are useful in that they enable the writer to get on and off the page with no effort, and they are perfectly appropriate in cases where acknowledgment is merely a formality. But in cases where sincerity is important, hunt for the right words, not for the ready-made expressions.

- Resist the temptation to exaggerate. Tell the truth instead. *Technical errors infest the proposal* is concise, but if there are only a few errors, then *infest* is inaccurate and reveals more about the writer's mood than about the fact. Avoid "crying wolf" with words. Don't write that something was *devastated, destroyed, obliterated*, or *annihilated* when actually it was damaged. Reserve *catastrophe* and *disaster* for situations that are truly catastrophic and disastrous, and refrain from using them to characterize every least inconvenience. Superlatives such as *excellent, outstanding*, and *superior* are like gold coins and should be spent sparingly; when the ordinary becomes excellent, "excellence" has lost its meaning.

■ Stay abreast of the language; remain aware of how words are actually used. Words are in constant turmoil and evolution, and the meaning of a word—the only meaning that matters—is the one in your reader's mind. Every dictionary says that *peruse* means "to read thoroughly," but everyone I ask thinks the word means "to skim." Who's right? That's the wrong question. The right question is: What does the word truly convey to the reader? *Skim* and *scan* are clear words; *read thoroughly* is a clear phrase. *Peruse* begs misunderstanding.

If we follow the principles of derivation, *biannual* should mean "every two years" (*bi* + *annual*). But that doesn't stop precisely half of your readers from assuming it means "twice per year," that *biweekly* means "twice per week," and that *subsequent to* means "before," "because," or "as a result of." Ultimately, what the dictionary says doesn't matter, not in the moment of reading. We all wish for an authority somewhere, someone who lives on a mountain, who would have the final say on what a word means and how the word should be used. But there is no such person—and even if there were, people would bicker with her. The best we can do is to pick the words we're sure will convey, use those words and no others, and say what we have to say with a minimum of fuss and bother. That's plain style.